THE AMERICAN SPORTING SCENE

ENDEAVOUR II AND RANGER

THE AMERICAN SPORTING SCENE

BY JOHN KIERAN

With Pictures by

JOSEPH W. GOLINKIN

New York · 1941

THE MACMILLAN COMPANY

PRINTED IN THE UNITED STATES OF AMERICA
BY THE JERSEY CITY PRINTING COMPANY

ACKNOWLEDGMENT

Mr. Kieran acknowledges the courtesy of *The New York Times* in permitting publication in book form of material which appeared originally in different versions in columns of the *Times*.

Many of Mr. Golinkin's works herein reproduced have been shown in a number of New York galleries, a few have been loaned from private collections, and some have been reproduced previously. To those collectors, dealers, and editors, Mr. Golinkin acknowledges a debt for earlier recognition; and he hopes the presentation of the works in this book will add to the constructive and friendly relations which he has always enjoyed in his professional associations.

CONTENTS

vii

PICTURES

INTRODUCTION AND ALLEGRO
SCHERZO

ONE fine day there arrived a postcard giving notice of an exhibition of oils, water colors, lithographs, charcoals, and crayon sketches of sporting scenes by J. W. Golinkin at the Sporting Gallery and Bookshop, East Fifty-second Street, New York City, and this ardent amateur inspector of art museums, commercial galleries, and private collections scurried around to have a look. There the artist was encountered, and it was discovered that he was, in another capacity, Lieutenant-Commander Joseph W. Golinkin (at this writing called into active service), and had served as an officer aboard destroyers in the earlier world war and after. One word led to another on such debatable subjects as art, war, football, and horse racing, and the dire consequence of that warm conversation is this book, a binding of art and athletics.

It seems natural enough to the partners in crime. Away back in the ages when Ung, the maker of pictures, fell to his scriving on bone, he drew for his cave companions the breathless details of their furious fights with the sabre-toothed tiger, the gory glories of their conquests of the hairy mammoth. These were the primitive sports of a primitive world. As Henry David Thoreau somewhere sagely remarked, the pursuits of the savage are the

I

sports of the civilized. Thus, with the crude drawings of ancient eras as surviving testimony, it may be maintained that art and athletics have gone together since time when the memory of man runneth not to the contrary.

In the "glory that was Greece, and the grandeur that was Rome," the bond between athlete and artist was close and cherished. We have marvelous marbles of boxers, wrestlers, and runners of classical ages. We have Greek hexameters still hailing the victories of heroes of ancient Olympic Games. In the statue known as The Discobolus —"monumentum aere perennius"—we admire the perfect poise and strong symmetry of an unknown Attic athlete of buried centuries. Who was Hercules but the Hackenschmidt of his time? What was Theseus but the all-around champion of his day? Ancient poets, sculptors, dramatists, and historians joined in perpetuating the figures and fame of their muscular favorites. Homer, Pindar, and Phidias mingled with the lithe figures of the ancient Olympic arena and made them deathless by artistry.

But relations between art and athletics somehow became strained after the downfall of Rome. Agile athletes, through the Middle Ages, no longer were looked upon as subject material for the masters of the graphic arts or the lofty writers of lyric lines. Happily there has been, in comparatively modern times, a revival of the ancient bond. All the more credit, then, to the followers of the arts who did not consider it beneath them to labor in that field "or ever the silver cord be loosed, or the golden bowl be broken." A few will be cited, "honoris causa," and Rembrandt might be placed first for his etching of what he called "A Golf Player," though the Elders of the Royal and Ancient Golf Club of St. Andrews would dis-

2

pute the legitimacy of the ball and club used by the Rembrandt player. The Dutch School produced paintings of wrestling, of skating parties and shooting contests. Racquet games were not beneath some of the early French artists. The English artists, of course, could paint scenes of the turf and fox-hunting without lowering their dignity.

Hilaire Germain Edgar Degas, whose artistic fame rests largely on the broad backs of ballet girls in oil and pastel, took time away from the "coulisses" now and then to visit the turf and paint racing scenes at Maisons-Laffitte, St. Cloud, and other tracks in France. Ignacio Zuloaga, the Spanish master, made his influence felt on canvas in another fashion. He was the man who was responsible for the appearance of Paulino Uzcudun, called the Wild Woodchopper of the Pyrenees, in the American prize ring. Being interested in boxers and other forms of primitive life, Zuloaga picked up Paulino in Madrid where this Caliban with stuffed gloves was just an "olla podrida," or ham-and-bean fighter, and carried him off to his castle by the sea to pose as a broad-shouldered, beetle-browed, native son of toil in a field of thick paint. Just to keep his hand in his own trade, Paulino became boxing instructor on the side to Tony Zuloaga, the artist's son.

When the younger Zuloaga went to Paris to study at the Sorbonne, Paulino went along as escort and, by brute strength and oaken endurance, gained some reputation as a heavyweight fighter in Paris. This encouraged him to come to the United States for further and much more profitable adventures in the ring. He was a crude and colorful gent of stubborn spirit but little boxing skill. Large lummoxes with small heart for the gory business

4

were his pet dish. But cleverer fellows peppered him and got away with it. Finally Paulino was incautious enough to climb into the ring with Shufflin' Joe Louis. For a few rounds he escaped unharmed through hiding his chin behind his thick arms that he kept crossed in front of him. But curiosity overcame him. For just a second he dropped his guard and lifted his head to get a look at his opponent, and in that second the Dark Destroyer nailed him on the chin. He went down like a stricken steer in a stockyard, was carried off—and that was the last of Ignacio Zuloaga's contribution to the prize ring.

Where the artistic and the athletic fields overlap, probably the favorite item is the great lithograph "Stag at Sharkey's" by the late George Bellows. It is held in high esteem on two counts: by the connoisseurs as a work of art, and by the followers of the fancy as an accurate and powerful portrayal of a breathless moment in a glorious slug-fest. Bellows did many other sporting scenes, oils as well as lithographs—a whole series depicting incidents in the clouting career of Jack Dempsey, the Manassa Mauler, who drew more than $10,000,000 in gate receipts at bouts in which he usually was the party of the principal part—and much of this artistic interest in athletics came from the fact that George Bellows was a fine athlete himself in his undergraduate days at Ohio State University, a boxer, a ballplayer, and one of the stars on an Ohio State basketball team that won the championship of the "Big Ten" Conference.

Even so, the inclination here would be to give the all-around artistic championship in the sporting field to another native American painter, Thomas Eakins. There are few phases of sporting activity that he did not put on canvas or paper. In oil, water color, and other media

5

he painted or drew boxers, wrestlers, swimmers, ball-players, hunters, small-boat sailors, and track and field athletes. He lived during the heyday of professional rowing and, from the canvases he left of the celebrated Biglin brothers and other famous professional scullers, rowing must have been, with boxing, close to his heart.

Overlooking Franklin Field in Philadelphia, where the Penn football team tackles its varsity visitors, was the studio of a sculptor, the late Dr. R. Tait McKenzie, head of the Department of Physical Education at the University of Pennsylvania. A distinguished Canadian physician, he had a keen interest in muscular development and physical activity that led him to model athletes in clay for clinical study. From that beginning he branched out into a far wider field of sculpture and won acclaim for his statues and friezes as real works of art. Many museums here and abroad now prize his work, and perhaps he might be considered as the greatest direct contribution that modern sport has made to the world of art.

On the other hand, Mahonri Young of the modern sculptors already had made a name for himself in the artistic field before he moved into the sporting field and fashioned, among other sporting subjects, the bronze statue of a boxer called the Tunney-Muldoon Trophy that stands in the inner lobby of Madison Square Garden in New York, with the names of the successive heavyweight boxing champions of the world inscribed on its base.

Apropos of sporting statuary, there is the sad story told by H. G. Salsinger who is, by distant relationship, of the ilk of the Ulysses Gunne of whom Kipling sang:

"He wrote for certain papers which, as everybody knows,
Is worse than serving in a shop or scaring off the crows."

6

Aside from being the top-hole sports writer of Detroit, Mr. Salsinger was and is esteemed as a connoisseur of art and, in particular, an expert on Whistler etchings. But sculpture is not entirely beneath the level of his eye.

Once upon a time—old inhabitants will remember this—there was a great ballplayer by the name of Tyrus Raymond Cobb. Ty of the Tigers! The Georgia Peach! He was a fiery figure in a baseball uniform, a terror at bat, a flash on the bases—and his sharp spikes knew no brother when he was sliding to a bag. He was the idol of his Detroit admirers and the devil with horns to the outraged fans of rival cities whose hopes he dashed by brilliant and belligerent playing in a Detroit uniform.

But in his later days Ty became the manager of the Detroit team and, because the club was not of championship calibre, he lost favor with the home fans. They blamed him for the poor playing of the team and, day after day, the former favorite was heartily booed by his erstwhile Detroit admirers. In fact, they practically drove him out of town. After all those years in Detroit, Ty quit the Tigers and went to play the outfield—at his age! —for Connie Mack's Athletics of Philadelphia. No one is more fickle than a baseball fan. As soon as Ty joined the Philadelphia club, the tide swung back in Detroit, and the citizens of that city recalled his great playing feats in a Detroit uniform. On his first appearance in Detroit as a player for the Athletics, he was tendered a ceremonial luncheon that began as a suggestion and ended as a civic demonstration. The mayor, the city council, the chamber of commerce—every person of public position or private importance turned out to honor the Georgia Peach who had done so much to spread the fame of the fair city of Detroit, Michigan.

In the enthusiasm of the moment, somebody proposed that a life-sized statue of the baseball hero of Detroit be executed and placed where it would be an example and an inspiration to the youth of the city. The motion was seconded and carried, "viva voce." It is Mr. Salsinger who tells the remainder of the tale in melancholy accents and with appropriate gestures. If it appears to be embellished a trifle, due allowance must be made for Mr. Salsinger's artistic leanings and his admiration for "all things beautiful and good."

In any event, the Salsinger story is that, the morning following the testimonial luncheon, Ty Cobb, at the hotel where the Athletics put up, had a caller with a beard. The visitor was a Russian who announced that he was the appointed sculptor of the proposed Cobb statue and he would be obliged if Ty would strike a heroic pose and hold it while the sculptor went to work. Ty fell in with the idea. More than that, he signed hotel checks for the artist's refreshments during the making of the little clay model on successive days and was astonished to learn, upon the presentation of the restaurant checks later for payment, that the man with the beard apparently lived exclusively on a diet of strawberries and cream. The bill for the strawberry festival, at hotel prices, was almost as imposing as Cobb's lifetime batting average. Ty paid it with tears in his eyes and resolved to have nothing more to do with art in general and with bearded Russian sculptors in particular.

The Athletics left town, taking Ty with them, and the sculptor went to work on the full-size model in his studio. It is alleged that, as a test of the fidelity of the work, a major-league umpire was invited or inveigled into the studio to give his opinion of the resemblance of the completed model to the Cobb he had known on the diamond. It is further alleged that, as soon as the umpire and Cobb in clay were face to face, the model quivered with rage and seemed about to leap from the platform to the attack. The trembling umpire squeaked, "That's Cobb sure enough!" and leaped through an open window into the back yard, making good his terrified escape.

However, that was months after the testimonial luncheon. With everything ready for the final casting, the Russian sculptor with the beard and the taste for strawberries and cream appeared at the Detroit City Hall and asked to see the mayor, who happened to be John W. Smith. This is mentioned to establish his identity and not for the purpose of concealing it. Smith was his real name. When the Russian had penetrated to the mayor's office, he said that the statue was ready for the casting and he would like to know where in the city it was to be placed.

"What statue?" said Mayor John W. Smith innocently.

"The statue of Ty Cobb," said the strawberry destroyer cheerfully. "Where shall I put it?"

The mayor scratched his head and said he didn't know where the sculptor could put it. He knew where he couldn't put it. He was warned against putting it on any city car track or within eight feet of any fire hydrant. Beyond that, Mr. Mayor had no official interest in that parking problem. He had forgotten all about the proposal for a Cobb statue and took it for granted that everybody else had forgiven and forgotten, too.

"I'm to get twenty thousand dollars for this statue," said the sculptor.

10

"I congratulate you," said His Honor the Mayor.
"Who's going to pay me?" said the Russian.

"I hope you find out," said Mayor Smith politely.

But not all the detectives in Detroit could discover who really had ordered the statue, still less any person or persons willing to pay for the execution thereof. The model languished some months in the sculptor's studio, and then both model and sculptor disappeared. Even Mr. Salsinger doesn't know what became of them. He abandoned them to their fate and went back placidly to his pursuit of Whistler etchings.

That doesn't nearly complete the roster of artists who, fortunately or unfortunately, were interested in athletes or athletics, but it's high time to move to the other side of the sporting gallery and exhibit some athletes who went in heavily or lightly for the arts. There is Bob Zuppke, the fiery philosopher and perennial football coach of the University of Illinois. "Zupp," who talks with a broad Teutonic accent when he is excited, which is practically all the time, is a landscape painter on the side. And he doesn't spare the paint! A teammate of Zuppke in the combined fields of football and landscape painting is the veteran Glenn Scobie (Pop) Warner, famous down the years as one-time coach of the Carlisle Indians, Cornell, Pittsburgh, Stanford, Temple University, and way stations.

Al Demaree, once a regular pitcher for the New York Giants, Feg Murray, a handsome hurdler from Stanford who chased Earl Thomson of Dartmouth and Canada to a world's record over the sticks in the Olympic Games of 1920 at Antwerp, John Borican, the Negro middle distance track champion, and John McLaughry, Brown University football star, are samples of athletes who handled pen and pencil, charcoal and wash, with professional skill and made it pay.

To clear up any possible misapprehension among sports followers or art addicts, it should be made known that there are—or were—two Rockwell Kents: one, the distinguished artist whose canvases are prized by many museums and private collectors; the other, a champion oarsman of old days who died not long ago. The odd thing is that the former champion sculler, seeing the canvases of his noted namesake of the art world and possibly trying to find a soft answer to the Shakespearean question, "What's in a name?" took up painting himself. Filled with hope, he sent a few of his small canvases for the inspection and criticism of the other and admittedly more competent Rockwell Kent. The canvases were returned by the party of the second part with the hint that the former champion sculler had made a great mistake in coming out of his shell. Diplomatic and artistic relations were severed immediately and the old oarsman took the rebuff deeply to heart. However, it is comforting to know, from the physician's report, that he died of something else.

The surviving members of the Chicago White Sox ball club of a dozen years ago will recall, with mingled feelings, the brief career of one J. William Goodell in their major-league company. He came to their spring training camp at Shreveport, Louisiana, as a left-handed pitching recruit. He made himself right at home and one evening, when the day's practice was over, he astonished his fellow players by setting up a music stand in the hotel parlor and placing thereon some sheet music of a kind not common in baseball camps.

As the wondering regulars looked at him, the rookie

13

whipped out a silver harmonica that had been presented to him by the Mozart Society of his home town, and, reading from the musical score on the stand, he plunged into the opening notes of the Overture to "William Tell," by Rossini. He played it through and then, setting up a new score and taking a deep breath, he assaulted the Hungarian Rhapsody No. 2 by Franz Liszt and finished that off.

It was a striking performance, but it caused some disturbance among his listeners. Upon investigation it was discovered that the protesting parties were not objecting to the player or his instrument but to the choice of compositions. They suggested a change from Rossini and Liszt to something like "Button Up Your Overcoat" or the "St. Louis Blues." In response to this public demand, J. William Goodell turned some more pages of his musical manuscript and played Chopin's famous Waltz in C Sharp Minor, which was his first mistake.

He made more. He was an early riser, and he just couldn't keep that harmonica from his lips. He insisted upon breathing out his artistic soul through its trembling reeds at an hour when rougher and less cultured athletes in the immediate vicinity were trying to sleep. A petition was drawn up, signed, and presented to Manager "Lena" Blackburne by the other White Sox players. It suggested two alternatives: sudden death by shotgun of J. William Goodell, or the tethering of the miscreant with the harmonica in some far-off pine woods. A compromise was reached by which Maestro Goodell was to play his harmonica only at short intervals in reasonable hours. During those intervals the other ballplayers usually could be found at the far end of town, holding their fingers in their ears.

14

GOLINKIN

But that wasn't the end of it. The gifted Goodell, overflowing with artistic impulses, burst out in another direction. He was also a cartoonist. He made crayon and pen-and-ink studies of his fellow players that he termed lifelike and they termed libelous. He pinned these sketches around the hotel lobby for all to see. One of the subjects, scanning what was alleged to be his portrait, turned to the artist and offered for two cents to punch him on the nose. J. William Goodell loftily rejected the proposal. He said he wasn't in it for the money.

But, alas, the heartless officials of the White Sox—crass fellows—had little interest in J. William Goodell's undoubted talent in artistic fields. When they discovered that his left-handed pitching couldn't fool big-league hitters, they turned him loose without a qualm.

Another sour note in sports was the attitude taken by two other ball clubs with regard to instrumental musicians on their teams. In 1931 the flamboyant, barrel-chested Pepper Martin of the St. Louis Cardinals ran away with the world series. His victims were Connie Mack's Athletics. Every time the venerable and kindly Connie peered out of the Philadelphia dugout he saw Pepper Martin, the Wild Horse of the Osage, rounding second base in a cloud of dust. Pepper, being a natural leader and a born guitar player—he called the instrument a "ghee-tar"—organized a Cardinal orchestra that he advertised as Pepper Martin's Mad Mississippi Musical Mudcats, famous for some years on the baseball circuit. At full strength, the instruments flourished by the Mudcats—for short—were two guitars, a harmonica, a gallon jug (empty; blown into to produce low notes), a violin (played blandly by Fiddler Bill McGee, right-handed pitcher, with the butt end of the violin held firmly against the pit of his stomach as he sawed away) and a set of traps consisting of a tin washboard, an auto horn, a flashlight and a bicycle bell.

This outfit performed notably at many public and private functions and finally reached such distinction that it was barred from playing over the air from a Chicago radio station because the ballplayers were not licensed musicians and members of the union. But did this music have charms to soothe the savage breast of Owner Sam Breadon of the Cardinals when his team slumped from championship heights and began to lose ball games in large quantities? Not by a jugful! He broke up the orchestra by shipping the players to different clubs and capped the uncultured climax by sending Maestro Martin himself to a minor league.

Worse still was the fate of an orchestra organized among the Philadelphia National League players years ago when Arthur Fletcher was the manager of that club. Those poor fellows—the Phillies were beaten to a pulp almost every afternoon on the ball field—solaced themselves with music. Possibly trying to stir them to desperate measures to win games on the diamond, Manager Fletcher issued an order that the orchestra should operate only during evenings following winning games of the afternoon! The musicians, under that dreadful handicap, naturally fell all out of practice, and their instruments grew rusty from disuse. This heartless attitude toward native natural talent may partly explain why so many of the performing musicians in this country speak good broken English.

"Shower-bath singing," of course, breaks out in all athletic camps, and some champions have been noted for feats of "bel canto." Earl Sande, the greatest of modern jockeys, Max Baer, former world's heavyweight champion, and Buddy Hassett, Al Mamaux and Marty McHale of baseball fame appeared as songsters on various stages and over the air. But British boxing annals have something striking to offer in that field. About fifteen years ago Frank Moody came out of Wild Wales to fight Teddy Moore for the British middleweight championship at the nobby National Sporting Club in London. To the utter astonishment of the dinner-jacketed ringsiders of that superior setting, just when hostilities were expected to start, Moody stepped back to the ropes and burst into some weird and savage chant. He explained later that it was the Welsh national anthem and that, in singing it, he was merely performing a patriotic rite and keeping to an old Welsh custom before battle. But the effect of the chant on his opponent was overwhelming. Moore never really recovered from the shock of having the Welsh national anthem roared into his ears before he could raise a hand to defend himself. Moody went on to win the fight and championship title with artistic ease.

About a quarter of a century ago there was in Philadelphia a boxer named Charley Kid Thomas who used to deliver himself of songs before battle, but not in the Welsh style. He tried another dodge. He would warble some soft, sentimental ballad like "Mother Machree" or "The Last Rose of Summer" with the idea of touching the heartstrings of his opponent and taking his thoughts away from any uncouth action he might have in mind. When he judged that his opponent of the evening had been reduced by the dulcet ditty to a point where he might burst into tears at any moment, the de-

18

ceitful Charley Kid Thomas would make ready in a hurry and sail into his man. However, from the pugilistic record that he left behind him, it would appear that either Charley Kid Thomas was not a particularly moving ballad singer or most of his opponents were stone-deaf.

So much for the historical background of the alliance between Art and Athletics, though it is admittedly only a sketchy account that has been offered here. The omissions are myriad, due to many causes including gross ignorance and vague forgetfulness. Apologies by the bale are being made ready for speedy delivery when called for. Beyond that, it may be pertinent to add that this book is the joint production of a former college boxer (the artist) and a former college ballplayer (the author). The reader is urged to bear that in mind and, filching persuasively from Shakespeare, to "eke out our performance with your mind."

BOXING

Ere the Golden Age of Dempsey, in the prehistoric day,
This is how the ancient heavyweight prepared him for the fray:
Sharpened spear and ax and dagger, put a new string to his bow,
And, discarding furry garments, gruffly muttered: "Here we go!"

For the rules of Cave Man fighting didn't hamper one at all,
And the ancient ledges echoed to the fury of the brawl;
Then the neolithic Louis, feinting deftly with his spear,
Crossed his poor deluded victim with a war club to the ear.

Though the purses weren't lordly, yet the fighting wasn't dull
When the crude Cro-Magnon hatchet sought the thick Cro-
    Magnon skull;
When the Piltdown Slugger stretched his man full length upon
    the snow
And made off with all the fishhooks of his unlamented foe.

Kindly note that at these battles by the mountain or the lake,
There rose no silly yelp of "Foul!" or futile cry of "Fake!"
For the game was on the level when the winner held the cave
And the loser was contented with a rather shallow grave.

IN THE first place, it's high time that elderly fight fans
quit telling those fairy stories about those terrifying
giants and ogres who roamed the canvas ring in the fe-fi-
fo-fum days of half a century or more ago, grinding the
bones of their opponents to make their daily bread.

LOUIS - BAER

They were fearfully ferocious fellows, to be sure, but if they were half as mutually destructive as advertised, it's a positive marvel that they didn't kill one another off in a hurry like the famous Kilkenny cats.

But the tale runs that John L. Sullivan, Peter Jackson, Joe Walcott, Sam Langford, and the like could have

DEMPSEY - TUNNEY

belted out a Louis with one hand while they were polishing off a Tunney dexterously with the other. It's all the more astounding because these roistering blades of the past days of pugilism apparently trained on wine, liquors, and cigars, delicacies that are barred from the

22

training camps of the pampered weaklings of today. And the hardy heroes of old fought forty, fifty, sixty, and even seventy-five rounds whereas the modern boxers complain that a fifteen-round bout is a long-distance event for which they should receive overtime pay.

So the old boys were wonderful and the modern fighters are a poor lot by comparison, sickly specimens of the manly art. And how do the tellers of these tales prove it? Simply by saying it over and over again in a loud voice and putting forward such powerful arguments as this:

If an old fighter went fifty rounds it was because he had the courage and endurance to stand up under terrific pounding.

If a modern fighter lasts ten rounds it's because his opponent can't hit hard enough to knock a sparrow off a cake of ice.

If an old fighter blasted his opponent down in a hurry, it was because of the devastating power concealed in his glove.

If a modern fighter tips over an opponent in a jiffy, it's because the opponent has a glass jaw or congenital sleeping sickness.

It's impossible to make any headway against such confounded logic, and the only way to get as much as a draw with the orators of and for the old school is to wait them out, say coolly at the finish, " 'Tain't so!" and walk rapidly away before the second blast begins.

Not that there weren't some tough fighters in the old days. There are outstanding men in every era—and in all lines of endeavor. John L. Sullivan must have been remarkably strong and quick with his hands. Peter

Jackson must have been a wonderful boxer. The bare-knuckle bruisers—the good ones—had to be desperately courageous to go on with their gory work.

Which recalls that one day a few years ago a train rolling down through the Harlem Valley came to a stop at a small station. One passenger gazed out the window and saw a scattering of weather-beaten houses with open fields beyond and steep slopes in the background. There was a general store with the sign "Post Office" hanging over the porch at one end. Several autos and three or four farm wagons were drawn up in front of the store. There were milk cans in the wagons. On a siding next to the passenger train there was a boxcar from which a farmhand in old overalls and rubber boots was shoveling some sort of ground grain—a mixed dairy food, evidently —into his farm truck.

The train lingered. The passenger became impatient. He rose to his feet and strolled out to the station plat-form, where he encountered the brakeman.

"What's the matter now?" he said. "Stubborn cow on the track?"

"Naw!" said the brakeman, acknowledging the bearded jest with a deprecating smile. "Just picking up a milk car. We'll get going in a minute."

The passenger glanced at the shack that served as a railroad station and read the sign on it: "Boston Cor-ners." He wrinkled his brows.

"Boston Corners," he muttered. "Boston Corners. Where have I heard that name before? Say, did anything ever happen in this deserted village?"

"Sure!" said the brakeman cheerfully. "We hit a load of hay here last summer and killed the off-horse. Farmer broke his arm, too. There was hell to pay."

24

"Boston Corners," muttered the passenger again, and then suddenly shoving back his hat, he opened his mouth wide and went on: "Why, it must be Boston Four Corners! That's it! What d'ya know about that!"

"What do I know about what?" demanded the astonished brakeman. So the passenger, surveying the sleepy little village and the placid rural landscape around, told him.

John Morrissey was a flamboyant figure in his day, a bruiser, a brandy drinker, a bare-knuckle champion, a ward heeler, a Congressman, a generous contributor to charity, and the man who made Saratoga a racing center and a gambling joint. All through the spring of 1853 John Morrissey had been challenging Tom Hyer to fight for money, marbles, or chalk and the heavyweight championship of the country, to which challenges Hyer had responded contemptuously by telling the future Congressman and State Senator to "go an' git a repitation" or words to that effect.

So Morrissey challenged one Yankee Sullivan, a bruiser of sinister background who had been beaten by Hyer but loudly insisted that he was a better man than Hyer and the real champion of the country. This Yankee Sullivan, apparently having nothing better to do, accepted the Morrissey challenge. Articles were signed, and Morrissey was to name the date and place of battle, the bout to be held approximately 100 miles from New York for $2,000 a side. Secrecy was necessary to keep the police from interfering with the plans of the lawbreakers and spoiling the proposed fight. When it came time to name the date and place, Morrissey swaggered into the saloon where the official group was gathered and said:

26

DEMPSEY - TUNNEY

"Gentlemen, the festivities will take place October 5th at Boston Four Corners."

So on October 5, 1853, the sleepy village of Boston Four Corners—now Boston Corners—was waked up by an invasion of roughs and toughs, gamblers and gentry, flashing fellows in loud clothes and a scattering of proper chaps with a red-blooded or even blue-blooded interest in·"the fancy." All adjourned to a near-by open field where the spectators formed a ring, the referee drew a line marking just where the warriors were to toe the

27

mark or "come up to scratch" for each round, and the stakeholder took a handy seat where he could pay off the winner with due speed and ceremony.

So they went at it. Sullivan was clever and knew all the nasty tricks of the trade. Morrissey was burly and courageous. They hammered each other about the ribs and head and wrestled each other to the ground. When a man went down in those days, the round was over. The fighter who refused or was unable to "come up to scratch" again within one minute was the loser. Morrissey took a fearful beating in the early rounds, especially about the head. He was cut badly around the eyes, and the "claret" was flowing freely. It didn't seem that he could last long.

But Morrissey was strong. He whaled away and raised big welts on Sullivan's torso. With head "bloody but unbowed," he kept plunging in at his opponent, and soon it was Yankee Sullivan who was "slipping" to the ground to end a round and get a much needed rest. About the thirtieth round it seemed that Morrissey surely would win; but then Sullivan came to life again, and for seven more rounds it was give-and-take, with Morrissey's backers beginning to worry much about their principal's stake of $2,000 and their own side-bets.

At the end of the thirty-seventh round there was a general wrangle in which Morrissey's friends surrounded Yankee Sullivan and informed him that his blows were foul, which was utterly unimportant except that the referee was calling the fighters up to scratch for the next round and Sullivan couldn't break through the encircling group of Morrissey backers to toe the mark. Thereupon the referee gave the decision to Morrissey, and the great fight was over.

28

LOUIS - BRADDOCK

Still wrangling, the principals, backers, and spectators lingered in the vicinity for hours and the constabulary, warned by the alarmed rustics, came down on the scene to apprehend the lawbreakers and restore order to the countryside. Having been, in some measure, robbed of his stake of $2,000 and almost ruined in the region of the ribs, Yankee Sullivan endured the further humiliation of being dragged off to the lockup at Lenox, Massachusetts, where he remained in durance vile for the night. The next day his friends came to the rescue and secured his release through due process of law, after payment of a fine for disturbing the peace.

John Morrissey also was caught by the constables; but, having been paid off by the stakeholder, John was in funds and made good use of them. He tossed a bundle of bills on the table and, while the constables were counting it in an absent-minded way, John and his friends slipped away and returned in triumph to New York.

That was the way they fought "in the brave days of old."

("Well, well!" said the brakeman, gazing around at the placid countryside, the stone walls, and the grazing cows. "Think o' that! You'd hardly believe it happened here. Well, mister, hop up! The milk car's on, and here we go. All abo-o-o-ard!" And the train rattled away.)

It was John L. Sullivan, the Boston Strong Boy, who

LOUIS' CORNER

made the change from bare knuckles to gloves for heavyweight championship fights. He won his honors the hard way, with his unprotected maulies. There were padded gloves on his hands when the crown slipped from his brow.

Just about fifty years ago, to the sound of a brass band playing "Hail, the Conquering Hero Comes," the great John L. swaggered into San Francisco on his way to Australia. At a gathering in his honor and for his benefit, the champion graciously consented to spar a few

31

rounds with a local chap named James J. Corbett, a former bank clerk who had taken to the ring, and who was much fancied by his San Francisco supporters as a fast stepper and clever boxer.

It was a dress affair. John L. liked to sport a high hat and a "boiled shirt." He couldn't be bothered to strip for a sparring exhibition with just another of those brash young fellows who were always wanting the honors of putting up their dukes with him. He and Corbett would spar in their evening clothes, simply removing their coats. So they sparred a few rounds and the former bank clerk, James J. Corbett, went away from the gathering convinced in his own mind that he could beat the mighty John L. if ever he could get a match with him for the championship. However, Corbett kept that notion to himself. If he had mentioned it at the time, everybody would have laughed at him.

John L. went to Australia and came back. He was still the Boston Strong Boy, the world's champion, the pugilistic idol of the age, the man with the mighty fist. When Corbett challenged him, he scoffed at the impertinent pup, the white-collar dude, the fancy man who would be destroyed if the great John L. fetched him one good clout with that terrible right hand. But the match was made for the Olympic Club in New Orleans in 1892, and "Gentleman Jim" Corbett, as he came to be called, kept telling his friends during his training days at Deal, New Jersey:

"I'll lick him as sure as apples are apples!"

Corbett's friends felt sorry for him. Nice fellow, Jim. A good boxer, a very good boxer. A handsome, upstanding young man of some culture and refinement. It was really a shame to let him go in there with a rough, tough,

32

LOUIS - BAER AT YANKEE STADIUM

BAER - CARNERA

roaring old lion of a fellow like the mighty John L. Sullivan. It would be no contest.

Well, those old inhabitants who saw it came to realize that it was no contest in the long run. But it was a dramatic spectacle: the burly Boston Strong Boy, carrying weight for age, vainly trying to hit this will-o'-the-wisp in the ring with him; Corbett mocking and taunting the exasperated old lion, wearing him down gradually with peppery punches delivered as the younger man danced in and out, and what was left of the great John L. sinking to the floor in the twenty-first round under a fusillade of blows. Even then the chief thought of those watching the dreadful tragedy was not that a dashing and debonair young champion had arrived on the scene, but that an honored idol had been toppled into the dust of defeat. For beating the favorite of so many years, the idol of an era, Corbett was derisively called a dude, a "pillow-pusher," a fellow who won a fight by dodging good honest blows and not striking until his opponent had been worn down from chasing him around. Why didn't Corbett stand up and fight like a man? That was what the disconsolate Sullivan worshipers asked in their agony.

When they first dubbed Corbett "Gentleman Jim," it was with a sneer. But Gentleman Jim lived long enough to make them change that tone. The fight followers

LOUIS - BAER

learned that it was wise for a heavyweight to use his speed as well as his strength, and his head as much as his heart. But hands, feet, and head combined were not enough to carry Corbett to victory when he met the Freckled Cornishman, Ruby Robert Fitzsimmons, at Carson City, Nevada, in 1897. W. O. Inglis, in his "Champions Off Guard," tells of the setting for that battle, with George Siler as referee and revolvers showing all around the ringside. Wyatt Earp, of western fame, and four henchmen with "artillery" on display openly, were in Corbett's corner and Bat Masterson, with four

35

more gun-toters, was across the ring to see that Ruby Robert was not imposed upon.

In the sixth round of the fight Fitz slipped toward the canvas and supported himself by grabbing Corbett's knees. Gentleman Jim was afraid to kick himself loose lest the Fitzsimmons forces yell "Foul!" He called on Referee Siler to haul Fitz off. Mr. Siler would have been right in the direct line of fire if the artillery opened up from opposite corners. He temporized, giving Fitz time to regain his strength and rise up under his own power.

LOUIS - BRADDOCK

Once on his feet again, the human freak with the spindly legs and the terrific shoulders went on to belt Corbett into unconsciousness in the fourteenth round.

Thus Bob Fitzsimmons became champion and then he, in his turn, bowed to James J. Jeffries, the burly boilermaker, who was promptly challenged for a title match by Gentleman Jim. No former heavyweight champion has yet climbed back to regain the throne, though most of them tried it. But Gentleman Jim Corbett came close to regaining his old crown that day at

36

Coney Island in 1900. Trained to the minute, keen and lean as a wolf, as clever and as confident as ever, Gentleman Jim went into the ring against Jeffries and for twenty-two of the scheduled twenty-five rounds he gave the reigning champion a proper pasting. But the one punch that settled the issue came in the twenty-third round, and it was Jeffries who delivered it. The big boilermaker, by accident or design, caught Gentleman Jim with a haymaker and "the subsequent proceedings interested him no more."

James J. Corbett fought again, but his heyday in the ring was over. By writing and talking and acting and going into various business ventures, he made a comfortable living. He was a great baseball fan. He played a little polo. He took pride in keeping himself in good physical shape. He had a friendly way with him and a kindly word for everybody up to the day of his death a few years ago. He was a fine man in the ring and out of it. And so, farewell to Gentleman Jim, a champion in more ways than one.

There is no need to add to the paragraphs, chapters, and volumes that have been written about Jack Dempsey, the Manassa Mauler, regarded by many followers of the fancy as the greatest heavyweight champion the ring has yet seen. His slaughter of Jess Willard, the Pottawattomie Giant, his short but hair-raising bout with Luis Angel Firpo, the Wild Bull of the Argentine, his two fights with Gene Tunney, his swift disposal of Gorgeous Georges Carpentier, the Orchid Man of France, his harmless bout with Tommy Gibbons that left bankrupt the cow town of Shelby, Montana, his gay days and wild nights were written, photographed, painted, sketched,

etched, and sung so often that anyone who knows even a little about modern prize fighting knows all about Jack Dempsey, the Manassa Mauler.

It was Gene Tunney, contemptuously called "The Student Prince" by those who liked their prize fighters rough and tough, who took Dempsey's title away by scientifically "boxing his ears off" at Philadelphia and defeating him in a return bout on the Chicago lake front, the fight in which the famous "long count" occurred. Gene Tunney read Shakespeare, hobnobbed with

LOUIS - BRADDOCK

George Bernard Shaw, chummed by mutual choice with Thornton Wilder and other literary gents, wherefore the fight mob had no use for him and were delighted when, after defending his title successfully in a final bout by polishing off Honest Tummas Heeney, a dull blacksmith from Australia, he resigned his heavyweight championship and stepped out of the ring.

Except for Max Schmeling, who was fairly good, the heavyweight champions between Tunney and Shufflin' Joe Louis certainly were an odd lot. Schmeling will go

LOUIS - SCHMELING

down in heavyweight history as the man who won
the championship lying down and lost it standing up.
When Tunney retired undefeated, Jack Sharkey and
Max Schmeling fought for the vacant throne. Sharkey
hit Schmeling a low blow in the fourth round and, as
Schmeling was stretched on the canvas, Sharkey was
disqualified for fouling. When Schmeling was raised up
by helping hands, he was the heavyweight champion of
the world. In a return bout later there was little harm
done on either side. The officials announced that
Sharkey had won the decision, surprising most of those
in the arena, including Sharkey himself. But he didn't
refuse the crown.

In the offing was the oversized Primo Carnera, called
the Ambling Alp, a monstrous Italian, probably a glandular case. He had fought off most of the other foreigners
who were cluttering up the country and demanding

chances to battle for the heavyweight crown. One of the distinguished foreigners hammered into submission by the ponderous fists of Carnera Carnivorus Horribilis was the altitudinous Victorio Campolo, known as the Tall Tower of the Argentine. Neither one, for all the bulk involved on both sides, had much stomach for battle. It was feared by the promoter that "oxen and wain-ropes

CARNERA CARNIVORUS HORRIBILIS

wouldn't hale them together." But they were pushed into it, to the unbounded hilarity of those who witnessed the tremendous event. For those who missed the massive sight, there is offered here a rather free translation of a remarkable document allegedly found by a sweeper in Madison Square Garden the day after the fight. To the sweeper, it was Greek. But to a classical scholar it was Latin and a stirring description of the previous evening's entertainment in the Virgilian mood, to wit:

"Arms and the man I sing (Arma virumque Carnera), who first from the shores of Italy (Italiae qui primus ab oris), lured by fortune and exiled by fate (fato profugus), descended upon Manhattan. A giant he was, as powerful as Atlas who bears the weight of the world upon his shoulders. His great feet covered the streets and his head was lofty among the clouds (inter nubes). His legs were as the oaks of Mount Ida. His was the heart of the Numidian Lion, with the fierceness of the Hyrcanian tiger.

"Ye Muses, aid me to sing of the great battle that ensued when Carnera Carnivorus Horribilis met upon the foughten field the Tall Tower of the Argentine (Turris

LOUIS - CARNERA

Argentinium) who came from the land of the Wild Bull (taurus ferus) and, strolling through the city, loomed as tall as the topless towers of Manhattan. Not since Hector fell before the onslaught of Achilles has the quaking earth trembled at such a battle.

"But first, ye Muses, tell of the lesser heroes who strove before the mightier warriors came upon the scene. Sing of Stephenus Hamas, a gladiator bold who, as a mere boy (puer parvulus), played among the Nittany Lions. Him Hannus Birkius, a certain German (quidem Teutoni-

41

cus), assaulted with fury while the onlookers sent up great shouts to the clouds. But swift was Stephenus, and agile, and in the combat was adjudged the winner.

"Next came Theodorus Sandwinius boldly to meet the valorous Cobb yclept Rotundus, great in girth, graceful as the Nubian giraffe, light of foot as the two-horned African black rhinoceros. Down went Theodorus when his opponent smote him as Ajax smote the Trojans. Now lies he low and dreams of verdant hillsides and sweet

LOUIS - BAER

purling streams, while in his ears there ring the melodious chirpings of a thousand sweet birds.

"Then came Publius Stanislaus Poredius to drive a foeman from the field, whereupon all lesser heroes retired and a mighty shout went up: 'Hurrah! Here come the elephants!' (Inveniunt elephantes! Evöe!)

"Cloud-compelling Jove and the Nine Gods of War sit by me. Ye Muses, guide my erring stylus. Now, Carnera, of you I will sing (Nunc te, Carnera, canam). War, frightful war (Bellona horrida), is my theme. The giants advance to battle. Let Mars be the referee, him skilled in the sciences and arts military.

42

"It was night (nox erat), and Orion the Hunter above the vaulted roof was climbing the starry heavens, girt with his sword-belt, to overlook the struggle and see fair play. Him the Gaucho of the Argentine (Equester Argentinius), Nullius Victorius Campolo, implored for aid in the great encounter. On the opposite side Carnera Carnivorus Horribilis called upon Apollo, God of the Golden Bow and the Golden Lyre, the great son of Jupiter and Latona, and likewise did he call upon Romulus and Remus and other titular Roman deities including Mussolinius Maximus, surnamed the Magnificent. Stand aside, ye pale and shuddering mortals, for the heroes have implored their gods and the frightful fray is imminent.

"Now sounds the horrid gong, and forth rush the great giants to battle. As Aeolus unleashing the winds from the vast cave, with Eurus, Notus, Aquilo, Boreas, and Zephyr sweeping at random over the harried landscape, is the unbridled onslaught of Carnera Carnivorus Horribilis and Nullius Victorius Campolo, one against

LOUIS - SCHMELING

43

BAER - CARNERA

the other. They swing. They grunt. They puff. They roar. Their lips are curled in snarls, revealing their cruel teeth. Their eyes flash lightning. Carnera Carnivorus Horribilis aims a great stroke that would have felled a forest. It misses its target by the width of the arena.

"Then Nullius Victorius Campolo shouts: 'Take that!' (Accipe hoc!), and lands a blow that, with a favoring wind, might have dashed a butterfly off a thistle. Carnera Carnivorus Horribilis staggers back. Now Apollo be his strength! Mussolinius Maximus stand by him! Help him Romulus and Remus in this awful hour (hora inauspicia)! Again the enraged Gaucho of the Argentine (Equester Argentinius) strikes his wavering opponent, swaying as sway the great elms in the fierce storm. This added blow would have crushed the stoutest eggshell, but Carnera Carnivorus Horribilis, after staggering back, comes in with renewed fury to assault his tormentor. Then did Mars declare a brief breathing space, and the heroes rested from their fearful labors.

"Now sounds the brazen gong once more, and Carnera

44

Carnivorus Horribilis swings his mighty arm in wrath. By some cruel mischance, Nullius Victorius Campolo receives the blow on his ample breast. 'Enough!' (Satis est) he shouts. But who heeds a whisper in a whirlwind? Again Carnera Carnivorus Horribilis smites his victim. Again the Fates frown on Nullius Victorius Campolo, who takes the blow on his cheek.

LOUIS - BAER

"Down crashes the Tall Tower of the Argentine, crying that he fears the Greeks, the Italians, the Germans, and the natives of all other countries, including the Scandinavian (Timeo Danaos, etc.). Fain would he lie there at ease, but the cruel referee calls on him to rise again. This time Carnera Carnivorus Horribilis, remembering the ashes of his fathers and the temples of his gods, smites him as Zephyr smites the nodding violets in spring, as a falling feather smites some grazing ox, unsuspecting. The gods have decided against Nullius Victorius Campolo. This last blow received, he mournfully bows to the will of Jove and the judgment of Mars. He sinks down placidly, at great length, and mimics pale

45

Death (pallida Mors), while the cruel onlookers laugh and Carnera Carnivorus Horribilis, the conquering hero, goes forth into the wintry night (sub Jove frigido) crowned with false laurel and wild raspberries."

For this and a few more Herculean labors of that kind, the glandular Goliath from Italy was selected to meet the heavyweight champion, Jack Sharkey, in a battle for the crown. Sharkey, of Lithuanian extraction—his right name was something like Josef Cuckoshay, though no two authorities could agree on the correct

LOUIS - CARNERA

spelling—had served a hitch in the United States Navy. With that seagoing background and a foreground of professional boxing, the astounding fellow halted his training activities for the Carnera bout one day to re-mark that he despised the rough fight game and doted on gardening, raising flowers. He was constantly tempted to quit the nasty boxing business and go home and revel among his tulips and yellow what nots. Such remarks from such a fellow at such a time were such a shock that they were directly responsible for the following

46

FLOWER SONG

The champion of heavyweights, a bruiser big and bold,
Who packs a punch in either hand to knock a victim cold,
Who smashes ribs or bashes heads of strangers in the ring,
Who bangs opponents senseless till they hear the birdies sing;
This mighty mauler of renown got in his hardest blow
What time he told his listeners how little flowers grow;
How larkspur clusters gleam at dawn, how roses look at noon,
And why the evening primrose yields its fragrance to the moon.

"I'm daffy," quoth Jack Sharkey, as he flexed a mighty arm,
"I'm daffy over daffodils; they have a haunting charm."
And as he smacked a sparring mate he said in dulcet tones:
"I've got the finest tulips anyone in Boston owns.
"It's tough this time of year, you know, to skip a rope or box,
"When in my garden I might stray and trim my hollyhocks,
"Or thin the coreopsis bed or bind the asters up,
"Or cultivate the columbine or double buttercup."

Ah, well! The world—as Swinburne said—is bitter as a tear,
And Man must tread the shadowed vale by pathways rough and
      drear,
And Jack must battle Primo where the steaming rooters roar,
Who'd rather gather roses like his golden Soleil d'Or.
Yes, he who dotes on dahlias fair must meet, in brutal strife,
Carnera (called Carnivorus) and battle for his life.
Sad trick of Fate! But Jack can take the purse that is his dole
And buy therewith white hyacinths wherewith to feed his soul.

Well, the heavyweight fuchsia fancier stepped up of a moonlit night (June 28, 1933) to defend his title against the elephantine Carnera whose feet were as big as pansy beds. The bout was held in the Long Island Bowl. It seemed that the lithe and leaping Sharkey had little to fear from the crude and glandular giant who was lumbering around the ring before and after him.

47

Sharkey had beaten Carnera in an earlier bout. But in the sixth round of this championship fight the Ambling Alp let go with his "bass fiddle blow," a sidewise sweep of his right that, coming up, caught Sharkey on the point of the chin and jerked his head back so far and so suddenly that the horticultural heavyweight felt that his neck was broken. He immediately slumped to the floor, buried his face in the canvas and was counted out as the inept, overstuffed, varicose-veined freak of gargan-

LOUIS - BAER

tuan proportions, Carnera Carnivorus Horribilis, was crowned the new champion.

If Sharkey had been consulted with regard to what should be written of his downfall, doubtless he would have said: "Please omit flowers." But without consulting him—he looked so comfortable on the canvas—the following fragrant farewell was allowed to burst into impetuous bloom:

48

TO A GARDEN PARTY

(With apologies to the late Alfred, Lord Tennyson)

Come into the garden, Jack,
For the fistic crown has flown;
Come into the garden, Jack,
You can sleep at your ease, alone,
With tincture of larkspur wafted abroad
And arnica odors blown.

At night did Carnera dance
And swing to a thumping tune;
And you lay there on your face
With your back to the staring moon;
With the twitter of birds for music,
And the referee's count a croon.

And here in your cherished garden
The wakeful flowers, in doubt,
Heard echoes of radio ravings
And trembled at every clout.
The white rose murmured: "He's down; he's down!"
And the lily whispered: "He's out!"

Easy there, men, with the body!
—There are thorns where the roses grew—
Carry him into his garden;
Pick violets white and blue,
And rosemary (that's for remembrance)
And give him a bed of rue.

Thus passed the former rover of the deep, the Garrulous Gob, J. Sharkey, from the heavyweight heights,
leaving the huge, unwieldy, thick-legged, and simple-
minded Carnera in possession of the throne. Along came

LOUIS - SCHMELING

that bouncing boy of magnificent proportions, Madcap Max Baer, the Harlequin of Hollywood, to beat poor Carnera Carnivorus Horribilis to a blubbery jelly in the same ring a year later. One dozen times Il Ponderoso of Pugilism went tumbling to the canvas like an elephant crashing into a pit. One dozen times he groped his bewildered way up again, dripping with gore, to face further slaughter. The referee stopped the futile affair in the eleventh round when it began to look like a case of homicide in several degrees.

The Great Big Baer had a marvelous physique and not a single serious thought in his head. He was the playboy of the prize ring, a natural clown, a ham actor instead of a brutal bruiser at heart. He didn't train. He couldn't be bothered. Life was a laugh, and he was standing on top of the world. James J. Braddock was a veteran who had retired (not undefeated) years earlier and had come back to the wars because it seemed better than being on the bread line. There being nobody else about, the plodding Braddock was nominated to fight

FIRST-ROUND KNOCKOUT (LOUIS - SCHMELING)

Baer for the championship, a selection that left Madcap Max howling with derision. To hear Max telling it laughingly, it was like turning a lion loose after a rabbit.

Nevertheless, tickets were sold, and the fight took place. Undoubtedly it was one of the dullest bouts in pugilistic history. For seven or eight rounds the disdainful Baer did nothing but walk around with curled lip, sneering at the plodding Braddock. Through these rounds Braddock was laboriously piling up points by pushing a harmless series of left jabs into the contemptuous face of Magnificent Max. When the Big Bad Baer began to wake up to the fact that his title was slipping away from him, he made a belated effort to do something about it. But the veteran covered up and nothing came of it. One dull round followed another to the finish, at which point the officials announced that Braddock was the winner and the new champion. It was a very boring spectacle from first to last and the ringside spectators who had paid as high as $16.50 for their seats were loud in saying so.

But better times were at hand. Shufflin' Joe Louis, the Dark Destroyer, already was looming large over the heavyweight horizon, blasting all opponents out of his way as he moved steadily forward. It was thought that the huge Carnera, whose hulk had been reconditioned in a hospital dry dock after the beating he had taken from Baer, might block the road of the comparatively inexperienced young Negro off the Ford factory assembly line who wasn't yet old enough to vote. But it was like a harpooner killing a whale. After sizing up his man —which took some time because of Carnera's mastodonic height, weight, and thickness—the lithe Louis landed a terrific overhand right to Carnera's face. As the young

Negro's glove came away and revealed the result of the blow, it was seen that not only were Carnera's features bashed all out of shape but there was mortal terror in his eyes. He never dreamed that anybody could hit that hard! He went down slowly, like a great chimney that had been dynamited. He rose up and was knocked down again and rose again, and was helpless and bewildered on the ropes in the sixth, with his broad back to his foe, when the referee stopped the slaughter.

The next man in line was none other than Madcap Max Baer, who hoped to atone for his shameful showing against Braddock by beating the sensational Negro. Such a victory would force Braddock to give him a return match for the championship. But instead of victory, Madcap Max suffered a terrific belting from the Dark Destroyer. He was bounced on the canvas. He nearly had his head torn off by the Dark Destroyer's blows. In the fourth round, down on one knee with his face a gory mess, he signaled to the referee that he had enough.

These striking feats of Shufflin' Joe Louis impelled this awe-stricken observer to tap out the following public notice:

LOUIS - BAER

OWED TO JOE LOUIS

Babe Ruth could bat; Jess Owens, run; Red Grange could
   carry the ball;
At this and that and other things, Joe wouldn't be good at all.
But when he shuffles across the ring, there's this that I can tell:
His left to the chin is something like the kiss of a three-inch shell!

Now, Joe looks slow with the fast afoot or the wriggling human
   eel,
And it has been shown that his own chin is not casehardened
   steel;
But that and the rest we well may skip, for this one thing stands
   clear:
When he lands that left his victim drops like a stricken stockyard
   steer.

It's true that a punch could flatten Joe—and the peril still may
   run;
For strategy he may not be the best beneath the sun;
But for zing! and bing! (hark, the birdies sing!) there is this that
   I insist:
He can pack the power of dynamite in the brown-skinned human
   fist!

Joe isn't as smart as Einstein; there are things beyond his scope;
He never will sing like a Melchior or speak like a Bayard Swope.
But of all the men in all the world, J. Louis wins the crown
For throwing a leather thunderbolt and blasting a rival down!

(And what a poet I would be, and oh! the songs I'd sing,
If I could put the punch in rhyme that Joe puts in the ring!)

What next for the Dark Destroyer? Braddock, the
heavyweight champion, by common custom would be
allowed a year's grace in which to make the most of his
title outside the ring. But a young fellow like Louis
had to keep busy. He knocked over sundry misguided

54

gents who probably expected no less at his hands and then, in the spring of 1936, was matched to fight Herr Max Schmeling, the thumping Teuton who had returned to the ring with the idea of regaining the heavyweight championship he once had held.

DROPPING DA' PREEM

When the Louis-Schmeling match was agreed upon and the date fixed, almost all followers of boxing felt that the veteran Teuton would be bashed to the canvas in short order by the young Negro with the terrific punch. But the odd thing about boxing is that, no matter how wide the apparent difference between opponents training for a fight, as the moment of battle approaches there is always an undercurrent of rumor or whisper that a surprise may be at hand. There are any number of reasons for this—a hint of a gambling coup, lack of condition of one fighter, lack of experience of the other, or any of a hundred surmises, inventions, or deductions that pass as "inside information" around the ringside. Furthermore, there are confirmed "long-shot players" in every game who boost the stock of the underdog to bolster their own hopes.

55

So there was a rise in the Schmeling support as the time of the bout approached. For one thing, Louis had skimped his training, probably feeling that "a shave and a haircut" was all he needed to put him in shape to beat an old stager like Schmeling. The rapid rise and uninterrupted success of the Dark Destroyer, according to some critical onlookers, had left him with the mistaken idea that it would always be peaches and cream for him in the ring. He was ripe for a rude lesson. And a tough, methodical battler like the veteran Schmeling, with a good right hand, was the man to give it to him. So ran the warning as the parties of the principal parts arrived in New York to weigh in for the fray. But, blandly trusting to the dark lightning dealt out by the Dark Destroyer, this innocent bystander registered the following opinion some hours before the fighters entered the ring:

They warn me of an ancient day
—I wouldn't know; I wasn't there—
When odds ran wild the other way,
And yet the Tortoise beat the Hare.
So Schmeling may, to my surprise,
Belt out Joe Louis with a blow.
I thank them for their warning wise.
I still like Joe.

They warn me that the Persian host,
In days that long are dead and gone,
Were 1 to 10 in book and boast
To beat the Greeks at Marathon.
But sunset saw them on the lope
(Except their dead, who couldn't go).
So Schmeling, too, may cross the dope!
I still like Joe.

56

They warn me still, in rising wrath,
That little David, brave and bold,
Unplayed at 8 to 1 in Gath,
Came in to knock Goliath cold.
The moral is that Schmeling's fist
May lay the Shuffler very low.
But stubbornly I here insist
I still like Joe.

In final warning, full and fair,
Of what may come when clangs the bell,
They tell of Braddock and of Baer,
On which I do not choose to dwell.
Despite the record of romance
When gallant long shots stole the show
—And giving Schmeling every chance—
I still like Joe.

Of a fine night in the Bronx they climbed into the ring at the Yankee Stadium and went at it. For two rounds the nonchalant and overconfident Louis raked the whole of Schmeling's right side with wicked left hooks. A couple of roaring rights to the Teuton's midriff gave Schmeling a touch of nausea. "He's a terribly hard hitter," muttered the battered Schmeling to his German trainer, Max Machon, in his corner between the second and third rounds. "Well, you're a hard hitter, too. Go after him!" urged Machon. Which the suffering but stubborn Schmeling did. In the third round Schmeling got in his first good blow and in the fourth he fetched the young Negro a clout on the side of the face with a right that floored him.

That was the blow that decided the fight. Not for the remainder of the evening was Shufflin' Joe in full possession of his senses. One Schmeling punch led to another, and Louis was rubber-legged most of the time. In the seventh round the Shuffler almost fought himself into the clear, and again it seemed that his sharpshooting fists would bring him victory. But just before the end of the round Schmeling caught him flush in the face with another right-hand swing, and he needed help to reach his corner at the bell. The twelfth round saw the finish of Louis for the evening and one other unexpected sight. So overjoyed was the late Joe Jacobs, manager of Schmeling, and so eager to salute his conquering hero, that when he leaped into the ring to embrace Schmeling

BAER - LOUIS

before thousands of spectators, he jumped out of his pants. His suspenders had broken under the strain. Mr. Jacobs hurriedly repaired this damage to his dignity and this discomfited observer went back to the office to tap out the following acknowledgment on the typewriter:

Lately I wrote in what might be called verse,
Mixing my meter with banter,
Louis would ready Herr Max for the hearse;
Burial service instanter.
That, to be brief, was the theme of my song,
Those of you know who had read it.
Query and Answer: Was I very wrong?
You said it!

Lightly I wrote that the Shuffler would bring
Maxie much damage and pain;
Lay him as flat as the floor of the ring;
I said it and said it again;
Stated it broadly and maybe too long,
Thinking I put it astutely.
Was I completely, astoundingly wrong?
Absolutely!

Naturally, the astonishing victory of the veteran Schmeling over the hitherto invincible Louis made a match between Schmeling and Braddock for the championship the logical sequence. So the contract was signed. Now, Braddock wasn't particularly desirous of meeting anybody in the ring except that it was the only way in which he could hope to make a large haul of money at one time. He was of the age of retirement. Aside from a large supply of courage, Plain James had little with which to defend his heavyweight championship title, and he knew it. The first good man he faced seemed certain to walk off with the crown that Braddock took practically by default when Madcap Max Baer didn't bother to attempt any serious defense of it.

Such being the case, Braddock's manager temporized. He decided to protect Braddock's title for a year and try to cash in on it in the interim in various small ways such as fight managers know: theatrical and radio ap-

BRADDOCK - LOUIS

pearances, exhibition matches, engagements as a referee
and what not, including paid indorsements of health-
building foods or drinks and articles the well dressed
man should wear in all weathers. So the Braddock-
Schmeling bout for the championship was postponed
until the following year on the pretext that the champion was suffering from a hangnail or some such serious
injury necessitating a long postponement of the championship fight.

During this long postponement Shufflin' Joe Louis
was back to the wars, popping over one opponent after
another in the devastating style that first brought him to
popular attention. With Schmeling doing nothing but
waiting for Braddock, who was in no hurry, the terrific
punching of the Dark Destroyer again caught the fancy
of ringsiders, and it soon became apparent that, to draw
a bigger gate, Schmeling would be shunted aside to clear
the way for a championship fight between Shufflin' Joe
Louis and Braddock. It wouldn't be fair, but it would be
profitable. Braddock probably realized that he had little

60

chance with Louis, but he would get much more money losing to Louis in Chicago than he could gain by losing to Schmeling in New York. Some convenient holes were found in the contract to fight Schmeling, and off went Braddock to Chicago to Louis; and, to give him credit, Plain James didn't surrender without a fight. He actually knocked the Dark Destroyer down with a right to the chin in the early going, but Louis rose quickly and, in the sixth, hit the bold Braddock a smack that felled

LOUIS - BRADDOCK

him like a shot duck. Plain James didn't totter, waver or wobble. He plunged. He hit bottom and remained there, out cold. And Louis was the champion.

In due time, that brought about the second Louis-Schmeling encounter, this time for the championship of the world and once again in the Yankee Stadium. And once again the Schmeling adherents were telling, only louder this time, what their man would do to J. Shufflin' Louis, Esq., who, they insisted, was made to order for their warrior. That required some thought, and the result of the thought was a revised version of the poetical

61

position taken at the time of the first encounter, to wit and viz.:

ON SECOND THOUGHT

They warned me of an ancient day
—Before the first Joe-Max affair—
When odds ran wild the other way,
And yet the Tortoise beat the Hare.
So Schmeling would—and were they wise!—
Beat Louis down. But even though
It happened right before my eyes,
I still like Joe.

They told me that the Persian host,
Who later ran to hell-an'-gone,
Were 1 to 10 in book and boast
To beat the Greeks at Marathon.
But sunset saw them on the lope,
As moonlight saw Joe Louis low.
Greek-like, Herr Schmeling crossed the dope.
I still like Joe.

They argued eke, in rising wrath,
That little David, brave and bold,
Unplayed at 8 to 1 in Gath,
Rose up to knock Goliath cold.
From this they judged—and were they right!—
That Max would land the winning blow.
But this is yet another night.
I still like Joe.

I've had due warning, loud and long,
Of what must come when clangs the bell,
And how again I will be wrong;
A state in which I often dwell;
Of how, once more, will Joe recline,
And how they'll shout: "We told you so!"
But here I lay it on the line:
I still like Joe.

This was one fight in which the ordinarily impassive Louis was looking for revenge and out for blood. Even against the boastful Baer and the loud-mouthed Sharkey (sometimes called the Garrulous Gob), each of whom had talked glibly and unwisely of what he would do to

LOUIS - BRADDOCK

an ignorant Negro and inexperienced fighter like Louis, the Shuffler had been strictly impersonal in dealing out destruction. With never a flicker of emotion displayed on his face, he cut them down swiftly but coldly. Apparently they meant nothing to him except as obstacles in his pugilistic path that were to be put out of the way. But Schmeling was the one man who had beaten him, and the Schmeling supporters had mocked him as a false alarm. Further than that, Adolf Hitler's published low opinion of the Negro race—though Schmeling had nothing to do with this—added another element of bitterness in the Shuffler's mind as he came up for this battle.

But it wasn't a battle. It was a butchery. It was slaughter, swift and relentless. A tiger couldn't have done much faster work on a tethered calf. Contrary to custom,

63

Louis was across the ring and into Schmeling's corner before the clang of the starting bell had died away. Ordinarily, Louis moved out slowly, like a huge serpent uncoiling. This was a special case. He was in a hurry. Before the stolid Teuton could fashion any kind of defense, Louis was on him with a left hand hitting repeatedly like a trip-hammer. Then the right came across. It was as if he had landed with a baseball bat. Schmeling sank back into the ropes, helpless, and Louis hacked at him savagely with both hands. Referee Arthur Donovan, wondering whether or not Schmeling was out on his feet, plunged in between the attacker and his hapless

LOUIS - GALENTO

victim. But Schmeling was perfectly conscious. Donovan moved out of the way and Louis, stepping in again as Schmeling came off the ropes, floored his man with a right.

The Teuton was so dazed by that time that, instead of taking a count, he rolled over heavily and came up before the timekeeper had tolled off more than a couple of seconds. Down he went again. And again. It was like watching a trapped animal being clubbed to death. It was brutal—ghastly—the fight game at its fiercest, goriest, one-sided ebb. Many sickened spectators were yelling for the referee to stop it. One of the Schmeling handlers hurled a towel into the ring, the traditional signal of surrender, but an illegal gesture under the rules of the New York State boxing commission. Referee Donovan picked up the towel and hurled it away. It draped itself over the lower rope on the west side of the ring. Then Donovan turned to count over Schmeling for the third time but, after getting a full view of the helpless figure on all fours, beaten to a pulp, he waved his hands to indicate that it was all over. It had taken Louis just about two minutes—2:04 was the exact time—to avenge the defeat that Schmeling had inflicted upon him in their earlier meeting.

Once during the savage assault Schmeling had let out an agonized squeal such as might have come from a tortured rabbit. That must have been when Louis, as Schmeling turned away to escape the storm, landed a blow in the middle of the German's back, cracking one of the "lateral processes" or short ribs jutting from the spine. There was some talk later among the Teuton's handlers that this "accident" had much to do with their hero's defeat. Zut alors! It was merely an incident of no importance. Schmeling was ruined by paralyzing punches to the jaw from right out in front.

Then the Dark Destroyer really was monarch of all he surveyed. But he didn't rest on his laurels. He preferred to keep busy. And he didn't care what man the promoters sent against him. He was ready to meet all comers, one after another. That included the almost incredible Two-Ton Tony Galento, the roly-poly bartender from New Jersey who was roughly—and the word is used advisedly—like a human beach ball. Of the globular Galento it could be truly said that he was almost as broad as he was long. He was bald. He had a round head set grotesquely on his orbicular body. No neck was visible. His fat arms stuck out like branches of a tree. He swung them stiffly, like wooden beams. He was a clown fighter in a way, unwieldy, with no boxing skill worth mentioning. Many second-rate boxers had pep-

LOUIS - GALENTO

pered him and taken decisions over him. But he could hit and he loved to fight. He could murder the big, slow chumps who couldn't get out of his way.

It was thought that Louis, when they met in the Yankee Stadium, would puncture Galento's corpulent carcass with one center shot and the barrels of beer that the roly-poly bartender had imbibed in training would burst out and flood the Bronx. Possibly Louis felt that way, too. He was nonchalantly moving in to the attack

66

when Two-Ton Tony, from away off, let go with a leaping left hook that caught Louis on the right temple and staggered him for fair. It was a warning that the Shuffler took in good part. He went to work more cautiously on this globular gent.

In the second round he pounded Two-Ton Tony with short, savage blows and one fierce smack sent Galento to the floor for the first time in his career. But the boisterous bartender came up again, and Louis had the pleasure of pounding him freely through the remainder of the round. It was good exercise, like punching the

GALENTO - LOUIS

heavy bag in a gym. It didn't seem that the gross fat man could last much longer but, in the third round, he landed another one of his left hooks and Louis himself suddenly sat down on the canvas. Well, well! Fancy that! Maybe the fat man would flatten the Superman! The crowd was in a frenzy of excitement. But the boisterous bartender, unable to catch Louis when he arose, had shot his bolt. He wheezed. He dripped gore. Louis began to cut him up again. In the fourth Louis hit him a terrific left that

started Galento down in one direction, and then followed it with a roaring right that caught Two-Ton Tony falling and completely reversed his direction. The punch turned him in mid-air and dropped him like a chunk of beef on the canvas. He climbed up again, but he was just a horrible, wilting mess of beaten bulk, sagging at every joint, spouting a bloody froth at every punch Louis landed when the referee stepped in and halted the festivities for the night.

Thus did Shufflin' Joe Louis, the Dark Destroyer, fight his way to the top and clear the ring of all serious challengers. Possibly Jack Dempsey was the greatest of heavyweight fighters, all things considered. Possibly Gene Tunney was the most scientific. Or it may have been Jack Johnson or Gentleman Jim Corbett who rated top honors in the heavyweight realm. But Shufflin' Joe Louis, though his chin was not of the strongest, feared no opponent, played no politics, cheerfully agreed to meet any fighter the promoters put forward, fought far more often in the defense of his title than any other champion before him and, as this observer viewed it, was the hardest hitter the modern ring has known.

69

LOUIS - GALENTO

BASEBALL

SPRING SONG

The southern sun was shining on the pleasant training scene,
And skies of blue were bright above a diamond set in green.
The manager whose autumn team had finished close to last,
With hope eternal in his breast, now called it strong and fast.
Two rookies up from Texas who could field and run and clout;
And the kid from California, why! they'd never get him out!
With a little break in pitching—it's the pennant. Wait and see!
(But the mockingbird was singing in the sweet magnolia tree.)

The gray-haired shortstop grumbled, with a proper touch of
*   scorn:*
"Why, I was pulling hits to right before these kids were born!
Okay; they skip around a bit—in morning-glory style—
But come a good hot day in June, I'll beat these kids a mile.
I've only lost a half a step in going down the line,
And when the clutch is three-and-two, they need a head like
*   mine.*
I'm just as good as ever!" Thus the ancient shortstop said.
(But the mockingbird was singing in the palm tree overhead.)

The tall and awkward rookie was a youngster blithe and gay.
He had leaned against a fast one and had knocked it far away.
"I'm sure to stick," he wrote back home. "Oh, boy! is this a
*   dream!*
Your loving son is going just like peaches go with cream!
The only guy I've got to beat has moss upon his dome;

70

I think he played for Troy, N. Y., when Nero played for Rome.
So ship my extra suit and shoes: I won't be home till fall."
(But the mockingbird was singing from the ivy-covered wall.)
The rosy hopes came up with dawn and flourished wide at noon,
And pennants flew in all their dreams beneath the southern
    moon.
From mascot up to manager, it got them one by one;
The veterans and youngsters had a little touch of sun.
The ancient soupbone limbered up, the youthful eye was keen,
And prospects were the brightest every manager had seen.
(And no one save a scoundrel would be spreading clouds of
    gloom,
But the mockingbird was singing where the oleanders bloom.)

Heigh-ho! What a life! The Chicago Cubs do their
spring training on Catalina Island. The Cincinnati Reds
once trained in Puerto Rico. The New York Yankees
once trained in Bermuda. The New York Giants and the
Brooklyn Dodgers, at different times, trained in Havana.
Dear old Connie Mack took his Philadelphia Athletics
to Mexico for their vernal setting-up exercises. Lucky
gents, those baseball players, old and young. Before and
after their baseball chores, which they enjoy as much as
anything else, they can loll in the tropical sun, play golf,
go swimming or deep-sea fishing, dance in ballrooms at
night, seek romantic adventures under a southern moon
—Halte-là! That recalls the frightened flight of Al
Schacht, the Clown Prince of Baseball, beneath the shel-
tering palms of a moonlit night in Tampa, Florida.

Bucky Harris, called the Boy Wonder when, in his
first year as manager of the Washington Senators (1924),
he led his team to a world's championship, was training
his Senators in Tampa one spring. They were housed
in the old Tampa Bay Hotel, the great crescent-shaped
edifice covered with flowering vines, famous for its seven

71

BATTING PRACTICE

turrets and later turned into a girls' school. Ordinary citizens, rich or poor, like to hobnob with famous athletes; and the guests at hotels where the ball clubs stop are no exceptions. But if they become too intimate with the ballplayers they run the risk of being involved in the horseplay that often goes on among husky young fellows of that type. One such guest, an amiable and opulent chap who had been a college athlete in his day, made the mistake of talking too much football while he was sitting around with the baseball players. Schacht, who was officially a Washington coach but unofficially a public entertainer with his antics that amused the fans wherever the Senators took the field, turned a trick on the football rooter that left him humiliated before a hilarious throng—and burning for revenge. With the connivance of Manager Bucky Harris, he had it.

Of a lovely evening, as the sun was sinking over the palms and live oaks to the westward, Manager Harris beckoned Schacht aside from a group of ballplayers and whispered:

"How about stepping out tonight? I need a partner. I have a date with two swell girls."

"What could be sweeter?" said Schacht. "Which way do we go?"

"You go one way, and I'll go another," cautioned Bucky. "It wouldn't do for the ballplayers to know about this. It would be bad for discipline."

"I'm wise," said Schacht, nodding.

A meeting point a few blocks away was agreed upon, and, since the Prohibition amendment was in force at the time, Schacht took it in stride when Bucky said to him:

"Listen! Buy a bag of oranges. They have gin out there, but they phoned me that they need oranges. Buy a couple of dozen."

They met at the agreed point, and Al had a big bag of oranges. They took a taxicab and drove about four miles out through the deepening dusk while Bucky mentioned some matters that left Al on the anxious seat, so to speak.

"We have to be careful," said Bucky. "We'll stop the cab a couple of blocks away and walk in quietly, so that nobody will notice us. You see, they're married women and—"

"Married women!" said Al, suddenly sitting up. "What goes on here?"

"It's all right," said Bucky. "Their husbands went North this morning. They're swell girls—lots of money, good dancers—"

"You're sure about those husbands going North?" demanded Al.

"Saw them off myself," asserted Bucky. "You don't think—in my position—I could take a chance of getting

73

into trouble? Don't worry. They'll be alone. Stop here, driver. Let's get out, Al."

They debarked in the dusk, paid off the cab, and started walking. It was warm. Schacht took off his coat. He carried his coat under one arm and the big bag of oranges under the other. They passed several houses set back from the road, and finally Bucky nodded toward a handsome residence over which the moon was rising.

"This is it," said Bucky, turning in and leading the way up the dark drive on tiptoe.

"There's no light in the house," said Al in a hoarse whisper.

"Listen!" whispered Bucky. "They're not advertising this any more than we are. But it's all right. Shut up and come on."

By this time Al had grave doubts as to the wisdom of the expedition; but for all he knew of his whereabouts and the residents thereof, he might as well have been in Darkest Africa. So there was nothing to do but follow the leader.

Bucky went softly up the front steps of the house and opened the screen door of a wide screen-enclosed porch. Then he stepped to the inner door and pressed a bell button. Inside the darkened house a bell rang loudly, giving Schacht a start. But nothing else happened. The adventurers stood waiting on the porch in the gloom. Bucky rang the bell again, and Al peered in through a window.

"I see somebody moving," whispered Al, and then in half a panic: "Hey, Bucky! It looks like a man!"

"No, no!" whispered Bucky from the doorway. "It's the girls. They're coming to the door."

74

With that, the door was flung open, the hall light flashed on—and there stood a great big fellow with a revolver in his hand confronting Manager Harris for just one breathless moment. Then the man roared:

"So you're the dirty scoundrel who broke up my home!"

Bang! He fired point-blank, and Manager Harris, clutching the pit of his stomach, fell in a disorderly heap on the doorstep.

"You, too!" shouted the avenger with the gun, whirling on Schacht. But in one wild leap Schacht had burst the screen door off its hinges—he couldn't pause to fumble for the latch; he had his coat under one arm and the bag of oranges under the other—and was down the steps and off through the shrubbery in wild flight. He ran about a half-mile down the road, with his heart in his throat, and collapsed in a ditch. At this point he made the interesting discovery that he was still carrying the oranges, though the party for which they were intended had gone up in revolver smoke.

He dropped the bag of oranges and thought things over. Manager Harris certainly was dead. The Washington ball club was disgraced by a dreadful scandal. He, Schacht, would surely lose his job and never get another in baseball. Furthermore, he was four or five miles out in the country, at night, without a car, and hardly knew which way to start for home. And when he reached the hotel, what could he say? Everything? Or nothing?

Plodding his benighted way back to Tampa on unaccustomed feet, the one thing that the weary and bewildered Schacht was spared was the trouble of concocting a plausible tale to fit the shocking situation. When he reached the hotel grounds and, coming out from under

75

the trees, started up the broad main stairs, he was greeted by loud cheers and raucous laughter from the entire Washington ball club, which was lined up waiting for him with Bucky Harris and the football rooter (who had fired the fatal shot) in the center of the hilarious reception committee.

That's just the tale of one city, a single incident from the crowded chronicles of life in spring training camps. In other years and in other camps there were ducks that were left swimming in bathtubs, young alligators that

were tucked under pillows of unsuspecting sleepers,
"snipe hunts" all night in the hills with starry-eyed
rookies left holding the bag, and "badger fights" in
which, of course, the object pulled out of the box or
barrel by the victim of the plot was distinctly not of the
badger family.

But spring training is just the beginning of the fun.
The teams go northward, and the championship cam-
paign begins in the big leagues. Which was the greatest
team that baseball ever knew? To hear Grandpa tell it,

77

YANKEE STADIUM

the old Orioles of the days of John McGraw, Hughey Jennings, Uncle Wilbert Robinson, and the rest of the vanished stars. Later-day experts will debate the outstanding merits of the Chicago Cubs that had the Tinker-to-Evers-to-Chance double-play combination and Three-Fingered Brown on the pitching mound, the Philadelphia Athletics with the $100,000 infield, the Chicago White Sox that became the Black Sox, smirched by baseball's worst crime, selling out to gamblers, or the great New York Yankees of the Babe Ruth and Lou Gehrig era.

It's still a wide-open debate, and added entries will be received from time to time. But the place of one team in baseball history probably will remain unchallenged down the corridors of Time. The Brooklyn Dodgers under the late, large, hilarious, and deeply lamented "Uncle Wilbert" Robinson, a crazy-quilt combination of great ballplayers and complete zanies who disregarded not only the rules of baseball but the laws of common sense. Their motto was: "One for all, and all for nothing!" By some natural instinct, queer players seemed to drift unerringly to the Brooklyn dugout. They regularly batted out of turn and often ran the bases backward. It would be difficult for any ordinary player to lose a game for his team by hitting a home run in the ninth but a Brooklyn player did it with ease one day. Two out, one man on, Brooklyn one run behind, the Brooklyn batter hit the ball over the Flatbush fence for a homer. It seemed to be a verdict of victory for Brooklyn that not even the United States Supreme Court could overturn. But the runner on base, lingering lovingly to admire the flight of the lofted ball over the fence, was passed on the base line by the heedless hitter who was in a hurry to get home to supper. Thus the first base runner was automatically out when the home-run hitter passed him, the game was over, and a Brooklyn home run had clinched the victory for the other side.

Marvelous men, the Artless Dodgers of Uncle Robbie's day, on and off the field. They had a huge coach who, dashing down to a subway platform one day, had the car door slammed in his face by a grinning subway guard. To make it more annoying, the subway guard, enjoying the situation, moved up to the door and, putting his grinning face against the thick glass, stuck out his tongue in derision of the outraged Brooklyn coach while the train still was standing in the station. Whereupon the Brooklyn coach hauled off with his ponderous right fist and let fly, smashing the heavy glass and knocking the astonished guard for a full loop as the train began to move away. The Brooklyn coach's knuckles and fingers were bruised and cut to ribbons, but his triumphant comment as they patched up his hand was:

"I sure tagged him out!"

That's enough to give a general idea of how baseball was played by the Brooklyn boys and, rather than go on with an endless tale of their escapades and idiocies, on and off the diamond, it might be summed up in the following confidential way, which is:

LOW AND INSIDE

(With an assist for Dr. Oliver St. John Gogarty)

Oh, boys; the things I've seen!
The games the Dodgers played!
How Manager Robinson turned pea-green,
Swearing his fate was hard;
Putting his hair in a braid.

79

Don't pester me to tell
What happened from park to park.
Don't—for I know quite well
'Twould drive you raving, stark.
Just thank a reticent bard
For keeping the matter dark.

The story if plainly told,
You wouldn't believe was true;
You'd say you were being sold.
The wicked might even smirk
At the Dodgers on review;
And I'd be sorry I spoke.
I'm all for spreading joys,
And having a friendly smoke,
And making no awkward noise;
So better go on with your work.
But, boys! Oh, boys! Oh, boys!

So much for teamwork. Now for the individualistic touch—and in that direction it was a disgusted Dodger, one Gink Hendrick, who announced an isolationist policy that was not only complete and final but filled with the old Brooklyn flavor. Gink was on first base, and the batter gave him the hit-and-run sign. Gink was to dust off toward second, and the batter was to hit the ball— behind him, if possible—to cover his flight. The pitcher pitched. Gink ran. The batter never even waved at the ball. The amused catcher pegged down to second where the outraged Hendrick was tagged out by six feet. As he arose from the dirt and dusted himself off, Gink turned toward his teammates in the Brooklyn dugout and, fairly seething with wrath, shouted:

"After this, it's every man for theirself!"

On this brilliant basis, three men stand out in baseball annals: Hans Wagner, Ty Cobb, and Babe Ruth. The

80

late John McGraw always insisted that "the Dutchman" (meaning the great Wagner of many years with the Pittsburgh Pirates) was the greatest of all. There was no doubt that the broad-beamed, long-armed, bowlegged, hook-nosed "Honus" was an enduring marvel on the diamond and, at a dinner held in his honor after his retirement from active service, this character witness was blushingly moved to testify as follows:

KNOW YE ALL MEN BY THESE PRESENTS

In the diamond days of long ago
There was a Pirate crew:
Abstein and Abbaticcio;
Adams to breeze them through;
And old Fred Clarke who played left field
And did the work of two.

Tommy Leach was a nifty lad,
Tommy could play the game.
Miller the lanky at second base
(Dots was his proper name).
Gibson would crouch to catch the ball;
Camnitz would curve the same.

And out at short was the Mighty Hans,
Bowlegged, bare of arm,
Who covered the ground like morning dew
And fielded like a charm;
He speared the liners right and left
To save his team from harm.

Hans was the man to field and throw
Or down the base line flit;
But best of all he could clout the ball:
Ja wohl! Could the Dutchman hit!
And oh! how the pitchers breathed relief
When Hans the Mighty quit.

81

Even so, and granting that John McGraw was an authority on baseball, he might have been swayed by pride and prejudice in putting Hans Wagner above Ty of the Tigers and the great Bambino of the Yankees in baseball history. McGraw and his Giants waged a bitter feud with Cobb when the Tigers were playing the Giants in spring exhibition games. One night it came down to a gory fist fight in a hotel room between Cobb and the much smaller Buck Herzog, infielder for the Giants, in which the little Giant was ruthlessly mauled. As for the great Bambino, he played with the Yankees, the arch rivals of the Giants for the New York trade, and thus the belligerent McGraw never had a good word—or even a civil word—for him. Furthermore, Ruth and Cobb were American League players and McGraw, rooted in the National League, had his blind side turned toward American League stars.

As between Ty Cobb, the Georgia Peach, and Babe Ruth, the Home Run King, too many disputing fans overlook the fact that Ruth was a double star. He was one of the greatest left-handed pitchers in the game when he gave up work on the mound to become an outfielder and the greatest long-distance hitter baseball ever had known. Ruth still holds the record of having pitched twenty-nine consecutive scoreless innings in world-series competition.

Tyrus Raymond Cobb was deadly at bat and a streak on the bases. He was a terrific fighter, with no holds barred. Though he never was a great thrower, his dazzling speed afoot made him a hawk in the outfield and, on the attack or defense, his keen mind and fiery energy often threw the rival clubs into startled confusion and ludicrous defeat. He was dynamic and unpredictable and altogether an astounding athlete. Yes, he was a great ballplayer. But Babe Ruth was more than a ballplayer; he was a world figure. His name and fame were known in lands and circles where baseball never was seen or known. Here was a Homeric character, Gargantuan in size and shape, outstanding on the playing field and equally famed for his carefree and colorful adventures in other fields. He was paid $80,000 for a single season with the Yankees—far beyond anything any other ballplayer ever had laid hands on for similar service—and drew almost a cool million from baseball alone before he retired. Being an object of public adoration, he had a vast income from other sources.

He reaped a harvest as an author for years by lending his name to a syndicated series of daily stories that were "ghosted" for him. He was in the movies. He once received a cheque for $25,000 for doing a movie in Cuba and carried it around in his pocket so long that it became merely a scrap of waste paper. In the long interim between the time Ruth received the cheque and presented it for payment, the movie company had gone bankrupt. He once received $25,000 for doing five weeks of vaudeville appearances in different cities. It was during the Prohibition period, and the Babe was not a Prohibitionist. "Au contraire." When the vaudeville tour took him to Chicago, a city in which he had many convivial acquaintances, he called in a bootlegger and told him to stock up the closet in his hotel room with liquor. The bootlegger filled the closet with cases of wine and whiskey. The bill came to $3,000. Ruth paid it. On this tour in which he earned $25,000, he spent $30,000. He was like that.

He received the longest suspension in baseball—he

was out of the line-up for the first thirty-nine games of the 1921 season—because he paid no attention to an edict issued by the Commissioner of Baseball, Judge Kenesaw Mountain Landis, and, indeed, told the dignified, white-haired ex-jurist of the Federal Court to "go jump in the lake," presumably Lake Michigan, which was handy to the Landis office. He suffered the largest fine ever assessed on any ballplayer, $5,000, for compound fractures of the rules of discipline and outright defiance of the Yankee manager of the time, the late Miller Huggins.

His adventures were hilarious, innumerable, and historical. In some cases they were almost incredible and in others they were utterly unprintable. His feats on the playing field were on the same large and colorful scale. He was greathearted and freehanded. He threw his money around with a lavish hand and was never too tired to greet his youngest or seediest admirer with a big grin, a hearty handshake, and kindly words. He was worshiped by millions, and he loved it. He went on the rocks, seemed to have made a complete wreck of himself, and pulled himself into the clear again to soar to greater heights than ever, this time with a better grip on himself and a wiser hand with his money.

All of which leads to the verdict here that:

You may sing your song of the good old days till the phantom
  cows come home;
You may dig up tales of baseball feats from many a dusty tome;
You may rise to tell of Rube Waddell and the way he buzzed
  them through,
And top it all with the great fast ball that Rusie's rooters knew.
You may rant of Brouthers, Keefe and Ward and half a dozen
  more;

THE BULL PEN

SAND-LOT

You may quote by rote from the record book in a way that I
    deplore;
You may rave away till the break of day, but the truth remains
    the truth:
From "One Old Cat" to the last "At Bat," was there ever a guy
    like Ruth?

He could start and go, he could catch and throw, he could field
    with the very best;
Hail, Sultan of Swat! (And the title was not the gift of a witless
    jest.)
He could hit that ball o'er the garden wall, high up and far away,
Beyond the uttermost picket lines where the fleet-foot fielders
    stray.
He was Bogy Man for the pitching clan, and he clubbed them
    soon and late;
He manned his guns and hit home runs from here to the Golden
    Gate.
With vim and verve he walloped the curve from Texas to
    Duluth;
Which is no small task, and I rise to ask: Was there ever a guy
    like Ruth?

You may rise and sing till the rafters ring that sad and sorrowful
    strain:
"They strive and fail—it's the old, old tale; but they never come
    back again!"
Yes, it's in the dope, when they hit the slope—they're off to the
    shadowed vale;
But the great big Bam with the circuit slam came back on the
    uphill trail;
Came back through jeers from the drifted years where the best
    of them go down;
Came back once more with a record score to wear a brighter
    crown.
My voice may be loud above the crowd and my words just a bit
    uncouth,
But I'll stand and shout till the last man's out: There was never
    a guy like Ruth!

86

THE RULER OF COURTS

THERE have been three outstanding figures, on the tennis courts of this country; William A. Larned, Maurice McLoughlin and William Tatem Tilden, 2nd. Larned was not the first but the last and probably the greatest of the old masters. He ruled in the days when swanky Newport, Rhode Island, was the center of the Smart Set of gay summer days, and it was there that the tennis championships were settled with high society looking on and the vulgar barred by mutual consent as well as by the scarcity of seats in the sacred enclosure and the high price of tickets. There was an aura of aristocracy, a touch of hauteur, to the game in those days. The courts of the class-conscious Casino were not to be profaned by the common herd. And in the last decade of this austere era, William A. Larned was the Nestor at the net, the stand-out champion who waited with due dignity while some knightly challenger fought his way through the lists—the tourney of the royal racquet week—for the honor of being baffled by Champion Larned in the ultimate challenge round.

Then came a larruping Lochinvar out of the West: Maurice E. McLoughlin, the California Comet, with a slashing, smashing game and a flaming thatch of red hair to make his rise more colorful. In three years Red McLoughlin dispersed the lavender and old lace trappings

of the upstage game of tennis. He brought tennis down
to the common ground. It was no longer a game for the
Four Hundred—not the way Red McLoughlin played it.
He made it a game for the millions, for the young fellows at the small clubs about the country and the youngsters just starting out on the courts in the public parks.

Thus was tennis happily knocked off its lofty perch
and put on a footing where the kids of the country could
go at it with vim and vigor. No longer was it a select
diversion of the society set. No longer did the man in the
street or the boy in public school regard it disdainfully
as a sissy sport. The way Red McLoughlin laid about
him with the racquet, it was a slam-bang, all-out, give-
and-take tussle that was just as much fun for the masses
as it had been for the classes before the kid from California came from a public park court to raise hob on the
conservative turf of the Newport Casino enclosure.

The shock was more than Newport could stand. Probably with a feeling of some relief but with an assumed
air of "Noblesse oblige," Society bade farewell, not au
revoir, to the holding of the national tennis championship each season as part of the glittering program of summer gaiety for the swanky set at Newport, Rhode Island.
The national championship was shifted to Forest Hills,
Long Island, in 1915, shifted to the Germantown Cricket
Club of Philadelphia in 1921 and back again to Forest
Hills when the concrete tennis bowl was finished and
ready for occupancy by championship crowds and players. Where it may be shifted in the future, deponent
sayeth not; but the sun will never rise on championship
tennis at Newport again, unless it is in some nostalgic
memorial celebration of the quaint days of old.

When the flaming Red McLoughlin wrenched the
game away from the patricians and brought it down to

88

the crowd, the kids of the country went for it avidly and made the most of it. With millions slamming away at it where only thousands had toyed with it before, something drastic was bound to come of the program. And the something drastic was William Tatem Tilden, 2nd: Big Bill from Philadelphia, for six full years the king of the courts of all the world. England, Australia, the Continent, the United States—with racquet in hand, Big Bill was monarch of all he surveyed. No one could stand before him.

Big Bill was more than a monarch. He was a great artist and a great actor. He combed his dark hair with an air. He strode the court like a confident conqueror. He rebuked crowds at tournaments and sent critical officials scurrying to cover. He carved up his opponents as a royal chef would carve meat to the king's taste. He had a fine flair for the dramatic; and, with his vast height and reach and boundless zest and energy over a span of years, he was the most striking and commanding figure the game of tennis ever had put in court.

There wasn't anything in the game that he couldn't do superlatively. His service was a cannonball. His ground strokes were lightning thrusts. His volleying was superb. With his long legs, he could cover the court in three strides. He was as light on his feet as a ballet dancer. His backhand was baffling. His chops and drop shots were feats of legerdemain. And for tactics and strategy he had all his opponents backed off the board. When Tilden was Tilden, nobody could touch him. In fact, nobody could compare with him. And King William knew it and reveled in it. He wrote for the newspapers and magazines. He trod the boards as an actor. He lectured. He laid down the law. He bestrode the tennis world like a Colossus between whose legs the lesser figures of the game ran about and found themselves dishonorable graves.

On the expense accounts afforded by the modern game, he traveled in style and lived in comparative luxury. Paris, London, Southampton, Hot Springs, Sydney, Cannes knew his footprints and his regal ways. With Master Justice Shallow, he had heard the chimes at midnight. He played bridge until all hours. He smoked cigarettes as one to the manner born. It was a terrific shock, then, to learn that one day, shortly after his retirement from the championship heights, he had lectured a group of openmouthed and innocent younglings on the virtues of copybook conduct, the benefits of deep breathing, early rising, modest manners, simple ways, pure food, noble aims, and all that jolly sort of thing. From the flamboyant and imperial King William, who had partaken of and enjoyed all the luxuries and fripperies that three or four continents and a decade of traveling on a generous expense account could provide in the modern world! Copybook conduct held out as the road to success by the Superman of the racquet game who himself, by right of eminent domain, had trampled on tournament committees, defiantly broken laws that were designed to hem in his ambitious and adventurous spirit, and kicked the stuffing out of some of the finest stuffed shirts bulging along the official front of the game.

It must have been a wonderful speech. But the context is lost to history. In its place is offered a substitute as William Tatem Tilden, 2nd, might have delivered his message in the meter and manner of Quintus Horatius Flaccus, with the famous "Integer vitae" (*Carmina*, Liber I. xxiii) as a model, with or without the permission of the estate of Q. H. Flaccus, deceased:

91

SARAH PALFREY

ALICE MARBLE

ADVICE FROM AN EXPERT

Eat but simple food; go for early rising;
Follow out my plan, daily exercising;
Then your tennis game you will find surprising;
So, too, will others!

Drink but water pure, not the wine that glitters;
Whiskey let alone, for it brings the jitters;
Sip not even one little taste of bitters;
Shun it, my brothers!

Thus I reached the top, and thus you should follow,
If, across the net, you would beat all hollow
Playboys of the court. Though they call you Rollo,
Stick to it cheerly.

Then upon the court, with some crafty blending,
Power, skill and speed you will have for spending.
When the wastrels sag, for a happy ending,
Ace them severely!

KOVACS

VAN HORN

Once we were beset, with the French besetting;
Threats from Anzacs, too, we were always getting;
On my upright life did they base the betting
    I would outlast 'em.

Primed with ozone pure (and with a speed a trifle),
Strong with simple food (and a service rifle),
Fresh from calm, sweet sleep (what a tennis eyeful!)
    Say, did I blast 'em!

Place me in a land where it may be snowing,
Or 'neath tropic skies, with the warm winds blowing,
Bring your young net star. When the game gets going,
    I'll dust his jacket.

Thank the simple life (and a service stinging)
That at forty-odd, with the loud cheers ringing,
I—King William still—on the court am swinging,
    Boy, what a racquet!

Aside from Tilden, most of the net stars have been
fine players but, beyond that, nothing in particular to
write home about. They had their idiosyncrasies in tactics on and off the court; but, in either direction, they

93

KRAMER VS. WOOD

were mild compared to the great King William. One exception might be cited, however, and he was not by any means of the Tilden heights on the court. But Alain Gerbault, not a score of years ago, was good enough to earn a reserve place on the French Davis Cup team, and his subsequent career, in contrast with the hemmed-in hitting he did at Auteuil and Forest Hills, set him far apart from the ordinary tennis player of the top-flight set.

Alain Gerbault, at the height of his tennis game, suddenly walked off the court, turned up his nose at the caviar and champagne provided by the tournament committee, and went the way of loaves and fishes. Discarding his playing flannels, he donned dungarees. He became a sailor, a lone sailor. He was "the crew and the captain bold and the mate" of the *Firecrest,* a twenty-nine-foot sloop in which he attempted and completed a one-man westward voyage of forty-five hundred miles across the Atlantic. Others had attempted it. Alain Gerbault, a rather small, thin, wiry and melancholy-looking French refugee from the high life of the tennis tournament circuit, was the first to complete the trip. He had read of a predecessor who set out on such a long lone voyage. Away out at sea, in such difficulties as lone sailors may meet, this predecessor had written in his log: "I am going out to the end of the bowsprit. Shall I return?" The answer was evident when his empty boat was picked up later by a transatlantic steamer and the question in the log was scanned by the salvaging officer.

In a book that he wrote of his own voyages in the *Firecrest,* M. Gerbault confesses that he remembered that incident when he had to go out to the end of his own bowsprit in mid-ocean with a storm raging. But he came

94

back even though there were moments during which, clinging with legs and arms, he was hanging headforemost under three feet of water out there. He was 101 days from Gibraltar to Fort Totten, Long Island, and for months he never saw another human being. His drinking water spoiled. He suffered severely from thirst. His salt meat rotted. His sails were ripped and torn time and again by wild winds at sea.

Racked with fever, soaked with spray and rain, with his throat swollen from thirst, short of food, possibly Alain Gerbault on the wild waste of the tossing Atlantic thought of his tennis days on the Riviera when during the luncheon period—and at the expense of the willing tournament committee—the club waiter or restaurant captain would offer the tennis stars at a select table a menu starting:

HORS-D'ŒUVRES VARIÉES   PAMPLEMOUSSE RAFRAÎCHI AU KIRSCH
OLIVES VERTES   CÉLERI EN BRANCHES   OLIVES NOIRES
POTAGES
CRÈME FONTANGES
CONSOMMÉ ANDALOUSE
CONSOMMÉ FROID EN TASSE
SOUPE À L'OIGNON, GRATINÉE (10 minutes)

Possibly the lone sailor thought of that the day he had to heave his salt beef overboard because it was just too bad. But the strange thing was that Gerbault, after sampling the sybaritic existence of the top-flight tennis player and the hard life of a lone voyager at sea, preferred the life on the ocean wave and his home on the rolling deep. He went on around the world in his *Firecrest,* and his own written record of his voyaging is something to make any tennis story seem "weary, stale, flat, and unprofitable."

95

ABOUT HORSES

In February of this year (1941), with German bombers dropping death and destruction on England night and day, the British Home Secretary announced that, for the first time in a century, the Grand National Steeplechase would not be run. Doubtless there were much more important announcements made by the Home Secretary that same day, but the banning of the great jumping race at Aintree—well, it recalled a five-thousand-mile trip made to see the Grand National of 1935.

The journey really started many years before that. It began with hearing and reading stories of the great jumping race at Aintree called the Grand National. Many followers of horse racing detest jumping events of any kind. So be it. *Chacun à son goût!* But the preference here is for the gallant jumpers over timber or brush, and Aintree, at a great distance, was cherished as the scene of the most spectacular event of any horse-racing year. Or of horse-racing history, for that matter. The lure of the Grand National was strong.

Still, Liverpool was far, far away from New York, and daydreaming rarely carried a man more than a few feet on a long journey. There was sadly recalled the old verse

about the man who never reached fair Carcassonne. Did the late Rudyard Kipling ever go "rolling down to Rio" in pursuit of his own expressed hope? Never. Liverpool was just as far away as Rio—or so it seemed to a dreamer in New York.

But a further course in reading could do no harm. There was an avid perusal of much literature on Grand Nationals of the past, including David Hoadley Munroe's big book "The Grand National" and Paul Brown's "Aintree" with its lively action sketches by the author and artist who made a career of depicting jumpers and polo ponies. Annually Paul Brown made the trip from his Long Island home to the Canal Turn stands at Aintree to get a close-up view of the Grand National jumpers going full tilt—or coming down hard—on the famous course.

The reading course increased the fever. Possibly Liverpool wasn't so far away after all. There were steamers leaving regularly for England. In the mad month of March on the North Atlantic there is no crowding in the passenger cabins. It was just a question of packing up and going, once a man's mind was made up.

Primo Carnera was thumping a huge but helpless young gent named Ray Impellitiere in the Garden ring on a Friday night in March, 1935, when along came Mr. Clem McCarthy, turf writer and radio announcer for racing. The slim, gray-haired, keen-faced McCarthy squeezed himself into a tight fit in a neutral corner of the press row and, ignoring the lumbering giants in the ring, said cheerfully:

"So you're off for the Grand National in the morning. Now, I'll tell you just how to go about it and what to do at every turn."

No traveler ever needed a more complete set of instructions.

"You go down to Liverpool," said Mr. McCarthy in his customary brisk manner, "and you see Mr. Topham at Aintree and present your credentials. He's the whole works, has been in charge for years—you must see him first. When do you land in England? On Saturday? Good. You can go right up to Liverpool and walk over the course on Sunday before the race. It's called Walk-Over Sunday. Thousands walk over the course on that day."

Since the race didn't start until the following Friday, there seemed little danger of being run down by the horses if a tourist postponed his walking the course until later in the week, say Wednesday or Thursday.

"By no means!" warned Mr. McCarthy, who had been to Aintree. "Anybody can walk Sunday, free of charge. The gates are open. And by special permission from Mr. Topham, you can walk the course as late as Wednesday. But it's a three-day meeting beginning Thursday and they won't let you walk the course during the meeting. So remember that, and be off with you now, and don't fall in Becher's Brook."

The instructions of the kindly Mr. McCarthy were grossly violated without any ill effects. Thousands did walk over the Aintree course on this particular Walk-Over Sunday, but the traveler from New York was watching some rowing on the Thames that day, down Putney way, which was still a fair distance from Liverpool. Furthermore, when the Aintree course eventually was reached, it was discovered that it would have served no good purpose to "see Mr. Topham" as Mr. McCarthy had advised, because the revered E. A. C. Topham, who for so long had handled everything connected with Aintree racing and the Grand National, had been dead for several years.

This tourist learned of Mr. Topham's demise in an art gallery on Duke Street, London, where there was an exhibition of water colors of Grand National scenes and horses of other years. The water colors were by Paul Brown of Garden City, Long Island, and Mr. Brown, wearing horn-rimmed glasses, a tweed coat, corduroy trousers, heavy shoes, and a friendly grin, was on hand himself and just about to clear out and head for Liverpool. When he learned the instructions that had been given to this tourist, he told of the death of Mr. Topham and pooh-poohed the idea that a man couldn't walk the course after the meeting had opened. He wrote out a fresh set of instructions, which were followed to the letter. Mr. McCarthy's instructions, which carefully had been written down, were thereupon extracted from a wallet and deposited in a wicker basket fastened to a post in St. James's Square. On the wicker basket was the sign: "For Litter."

CORINTHIAN

Mr. Brown's instructions were to return to the hotel, pack a few things in a small grip, buy a raincoat—absolutely necessary—bring an extra pair of old trousers for walking the course, an extra pair of heavy shoes for ditto, wire immediately to Mr. D. M. Wood, Clerk of the Course at Aintree, for a special badge admitting bearer to all parts of the grounds, wire the Queen Hotel at Chester for a room which they would not have but they might put a cot up for him somewhere, meet Mr. Brown himself at the Paddington Station in time to catch the 2:10 train that very afternoon—and Westward ho! for the Aintree country.

It was a rush order for a stranger in a strange land, but it's astonishing how much can be done if it has to be done and no questions asked. The trip down to Chester this fine Wednesday afternoon was delightful. Three stout farmers came into the compartment at Leamington and gave the American voyagers a running account of football affairs and cup tie prospects until the mountains of Wales loomed up in the twilight to the west and the train pulled into Chester. The farmers also had their

HUNT TEAMS

ideas on what would happen in the running of the Grand National and expressed them in broad accents.

Thus did the travelers come into the pleasant section that is watered by the river Dee, by which lived the legendary happy miller, and to the ancient walled town of Chester, one of the *castra,* or camps, of the Romans. It turned out, as Mr. Brown had hinted, that the Queen Hotel didn't have a room to spare for the late-comer. Everything in the Grand National area is reserved for months ahead. But, also as Mr. Brown had hinted, they could put up one more cot, and this one they put up in Mr. Brown's room. He bore up under this imposition better than could have been expected.

Upon visiting the hotel bar for a trifle to celebrate the success of the trip that far, it was discovered that the Irish brigade—enthusiastic horsemen, strong for the jumpers—had arrived some hours earlier; and there was much conversation about Irish jumpers and English riders before it was time to turn in. Then the next morning there was a letter, short but sweet, from the obliging Mr. D. M. Wood, Clerk of the Course for Aintree, with a neat green badge that entitled the bearer to all the privileges of the grounds, including the right to walk over the Grand National course that very morning, which was Thursday and the opening day of the meeting. Harking back, it was a relief to find Mr. Clem McCarthy wrong again, and something of a pleasure, too, because in turf matters he is so confoundedly right most of the time.

After a hurried breakfast, an early train was caught for Birkenhead, the ferry trip across the Mersey was made under a warm and bright spring sky, Liverpool was given a hasty and insufficient look, and at Exchange

Station a suburban train was boarded with the feeling of a pilgrim approaching a shrine. Aintree was about twelve minutes away. After years of dreaming!

Thunder and turf! What's the use in trying to hide it? Stepping off the train at Aintree was a triple-dashed thrill, and no mistake. The rear of the great disjointed grandstand loomed up as the train pulled into the station. It was built in about half a dozen sections at different times, and the sections are not quite uniform in height or depth. The whole thing is called the County Stands or "County" for short. One of the favorite places for viewing the big race is "top row County."

Going in through the main entrance to the course, which is just a few steps from the railroad station, the visitor sees a long sweep of green turf bordered by a set of white rail leading away toward some low hills on the horizon.

"That's it," said Guest Conductor Paul Brown with a wave of his hand. "The start of the Grand National course—straightaway to Becher's Brook."

At last! The sun was bright. The weather was warm. The grass was a luscious green. The fences were dazzlingly white by contrast. Fruit trees and thorn hedges were breaking into blossom and "March made sweet the weather, with daffodil and starling, and hours of fruitful breath." And straight down that wonderful sweep of green turf was Becher's Brook, where the gallant captain with the magnificent black whiskers had gone overboard almost a century ago to make turf history. The command was: Forward! The time-honored rite of walking the course was under way.

Some discoveries were made. Imprimis, most of the Grand National course lies outside the ordinary Aintree

103

flat racing grounds. The jumpers start inside the regular enclosure, go out one gate, make a circuit of "the country," as it is called, dash back into the regular enclosure by another gate, pass in front of the grandstand and—in the Grand National, at least—go off again on a second circuit of the same. Secondly, a public road—the Melling Road, with plenty of traffic on it—parallels the fence of the regular enclosure and cuts directly across the Grand National trail between the start and the first jump on one side and between the twelfth and thirteenth fences on the other side. On Grand National days the "bobbies" hold up traffic at race-time and the lucky ones are those Melling Road lorry drivers or autoists who are marooned temporarily inside the course. They have a central view of the great race free of charge. The Melling Road is hard pavement but where the steeplechasers cross it there is spread a heavy layer of tanbark for the occasion. Incidentally, and for American guidance, Becher is pronounced Bee-cher by the natives, who should know.

Now for the course itself. The starting run is slightly downhill. There are six fences straightaway, the sixth being Becher's Brook. The first two fences are just thorn hedges thickened and stiffened with matted brush. The third fence is the first of the "Liverpool yawners." A

104

"Liverpool yawner" is not something to be taken sleepily. It looks like a long golf trap without sand in it, backed by a ghastly stiff fence. The fence itself varies between 4 feet 6 and 5 feet 3 in height, and in front of it is this trench—6 feet wide and 3 feet deep, with timber insets to keep the trench from crumbling under the cavalry attack.

It isn't the height of the Aintree fences that makes it a hazardous ride on horseback; it's the "broad jumping" that goes with clearing the obstacles—that and the sudden swerves in direction that horse and man must make in unison after taking a stiff jump "flying." At Becher's Brook, for instance, the take-off is innocent-looking enough. It's the landing beyond that makes or mars. The fence itself, from the rushing side, doesn't look like much, and Becher's Brook is just a thin little trickle of water. But going over that jump is something like going off a cliff. The ground falls away so sharply that there's a twelve-foot drop from the top of the fence to the immortal Becher's Brook lurking in the lee of the fence. The bank comes up sharply again on the far side, but only a horse that makes a "flying broad jump" out of it can reach a safe landing ground and keep going. That's why Becher's Brook is such a graveyard of hopes on the second lap; most of the surviving horses are too tired to clear the horizontal distance that will bring them to safety on the far side. A short jump means a great drop and probably a ruinous one.

No sooner is Becher's Brook cleared—if at all!—than horses and riders have to swerve left-handed, take the next fence with a rush, swerve to the left again, and go over the jump at the Canal Turn. There the course makes a square left turn, exactly like a street corner, and

106

away they go for Valentine's Brook (Becher's Brook that has changed its name in the short journey across the course), Anchor Bridge, into the regular Aintree enclosure for the jumps in front of the grandstand and so on around again.

If the horses didn't turn sharp left at the Canal Turn they actually would plunge into a canal. It's a real one in working order. Backed against the canal are the Canal Turn stands, with one exception the best place from which to witness the actual jumping feats of the horses in this great contest. "County" is too far away. In the twice-around race, the spectators in the great main stands get a close view of only seven of the thirty-one jumps that must be taken to complete the course. Twenty-four of the jumps are "in the country," the outer sector beyond Melling Road, and for a sight of the horses going over these obstacles the Canal Turn stands afford the best lodging place during the race. With the one exception as stated. That exception is a small brick edifice just beyond the Canal Turn stands. It looks like a railway signal tower with a plate-glass front to the upper section facing the racing ground. This is the private and lofty perch of Lord Sefton and honored guests, all the Aintree ground—and more—being owned by the Sefton family.

The pilgrimage continued past Lord Sefton's "private box," up the course and into the flat racing enclosure again where, in full view of the grandstand, are those famous jumps, "the Chair"—named for a rectangular iron grating standing like a pulpit at one side of the jump—and the water hazard after which the "Liverpools" in this country have been named. And so, with little more than casual glances at the racing events of that

107

afternoon, back to Chester for the night and again, in the taproom, much talk of the great event of the morrow.

"Morn in the white wake of the morning star came furrowing all the orient into gold." So sang Tennyson, and this was his England. Armed with box lunches, the expedition set out again from Chester, crossed the Mersey where the great ships were in their docks, and at precisely ten A.M. the train for Aintree was boarded at Exchange Station in Liverpool. The Grand National was scheduled for 3:15 in the afternoon, but only the Prince of Wales could arrive at a late hour and hope for a seat. Except for the boxes in the main grandstand, there are no reserved seats at Aintree. First come, first

served, even in the clubhouse section where the seats cost $7.50; but out "in the country," where many thousands line up along the course or mill about in the infield, admission is only a shilling.

By adding four more shillings to that modest entrance fee, a visitor may take a seat in the Canal Turn stands—if he gets there in time! Those stands, no bigger than the bleacher section at the Polo Grounds in New York, are thrown open at eleven A.M. and filled in fifteen minutes, or as fast as the applicants can pay their four shil-

108

lings apiece and enter. Led by Guest Conductor Paul Brown, the small party from Chester was right by the wicket at eleven A.M. and thus secured a position just one row from the top of the stand.

Four hours to wait. But it was vastly entertaining. Tramping down the course to the Canal Turn of this sunny spring day, we noted that kingcups were blooming in the infield, primroses were out along the moist banks of Becher's Brook and, flushed out of the grass by invading feet, skylarks were singing clearly in the blue sky overhead. In appreciation of the grand scene and the flood of liquid notes overhead, it was impossible to keep from whispering, "Hail to thee, blithe spirit!"

The bookmakers were putting up their stands and their signs in various locations around the course. Once in place, they clamored for bets like Coney Island barkers inviting the public to witness an extraordinary show for a dime, ten cents, the tenth part of a dollar. They wore loud costumes and had voices to match. Touts were hawking their "special tips" for as little as a penny and, when business was dull in that line for a moment, one of the touts indignantly asked where were the "spoortsmen" that Old England once produced.

Fakers, sleight-of-hand artists, wandering minstrels, and exhibitionists of all kinds played for the attention and largess of the waiting thousands along the course. There was a one-legged man who did a jumping stunt. He had his uprights and his crossbar in place. He would hobble up to the bar with his crutch under one arm and discard the crutch as he made his leap. For a penny he would jump 3 feet 6 inches. For tuppence he would jump 3 inches higher. For sixpence he would clear the bar at 4 feet, and for a shilling he would try 4 feet 6, which he explained was his Grand National jump. Nobody bid him up that high.

The occupants of the Canal Turn stands came equipped with blankets and raincoats and basket lunches and books and set themselves for the hours of observation, conversation and, in some cases, steady reading. One chubby half-grown boy, with a cricket cap perched on his blond head, was immersed in a book. A quick glance at the title disclosed the book as "King Solomon's Mines," the revered Rider Haggard thriller for juveniles. Wishing to know whether the classic was as deeply appreciated in Old England as it was in Young America, I asked the boy what he thought of the thing. "Oh, sir," he piped—and this is the solemn truth—"it's a jolly good book!" In return for which even a wanderer from America knew enough to say: "Dash my buttons if it isn't!"

About noon a long parade of "bobbies" came down from Melling Road, dropping two men at each fence and stationing others, with their long coats, high helmets, and tight chinstraps, along the rail between the jumps. There were mounted police trotting about the infield, too. The two "bobbies" at each fence were furnished with a stretcher, all ready for some Grand National rider who went down and couldn't get to his feet again under his own steam. The "bobbies" also were furnished with fire extinguishers and two flags, one red and one yellow. The fire extinguishers were to put out flames in case any fanatic attempted to spoil the great day by rushing out and throwing petrol on the brush fences. In the days of "Suffragette" disorders the fire peril was a reality and led to one fatal accident. The red and yellow flags were for signaling purposes. If a horse was hurt, the waving of the red flag brought the horse ambulance and a veter-

111

inary. If a jockey was hurt, the yellow flag was waved and hasty steps were taken to the rescue.

A bit later the police at the fences were reinforced by uniformed men from the Royal Army Medical Corps, and it was noticed that the detachments at Becher's Brook, the Canal Turn, and Valentine's Brook were extra heavy. Thus the hours of waiting passed with watching this and that and listening to the banjo, accordion, and cornet players who were strolling about, bidding for pennies. But the police began to harry and chivvy these chaps, wanting them out of the way because it was getting late and the Prince of Wales would be coming down soon. Across the course, above Becher's Brook, was a big railroad yard. The sloping banks were black with spectators. The County stands, in the distance, were filled to overflowing. Thousands of enthusiasts in all sorts of costumes and of all classes and previous conditions of servitude were crowded as close to the course as they could get and as far in the distance as the eye

112

could see. A hare suddenly popped up in the infield, and some Liverpool lads took after it with hoots and shouts.

Suddenly there was a bustle, and word spread quickly through the vast throng. The Prince of Wales was arriving to join the Sefton party in the watchtower beside the canal. Two gorgeous limousines tooled up and stopped on the road just across the canal in the rear of the Canal Turn stands. A special footbridge had been thrown across the canal. The well known figure of the then Prince of Wales (now the Duke of Windsor) emerged from the first limousine and crossed over the bridge, waving a black derby in answer to the salute of the crowd.

It's race time now—3:15 to the dot. Look away up yonder, between the big refreshment tent and the flag-pole to the left of the County stands. Yes, that moving mass of color is the Grand National field at the starting gate. Twenty-seven starters; no scratches. It won't be long now. Steady, the Buffs! They're still moving about— Wait! look! They're off! The Grand National is under way.

Down they come, sweeping like a cavalry charge. They pour over the first fence in waves and— Look! Three— four riderless horses already! Four more jumps taken almost as quickly as it takes to mention it, and the great leap at Becher's Brook is cleared—by some! One—two— three horses are rolling on the sloping bank. One riderless horse comes trotting across the course in the ditch itself. The police are pulling jockeys—fallen men—out of the way, clutching them under the armpits and hauling them under the inside rail.

The thundering herd suddenly pops over the fence at the Canal Turn, whirls with a great shouting, a pounding of hoofs and a creaking of leather and goes galloping past the Canal Turn stands. Where's Golden Miller, the shining favorite? If the favorite wins, the rumor is that the bankrupt bookies will throw themselves into the neighboring canal in a body. Who's that in front? Why, it's Pete Bostwick riding his own Castle Irwell. Go it, Pete! Wouldn't it be great for an American amateur rider to win with his own horse at Aintree? There's Golden Miller with that bunch behind the leader. Thomond II is there. That gray is good old Uncle Batt, always running in the Grand National, never winning. Reynoldstown, Blue Prince—one after another they thud by and rush for Valentine's Brook. There's a roar from the crowd just beyond the jump. Golden Miller is going riderless up the course. Jockey G. Wilson and Golden Miller went up to the fence together but were some yards apart when they came down. The bookies are saved.

Now the pack disappears from sight up the course, but a moving volume of cheering, keeping pace with the leaders, tells the waiting thousands in the Canal Turn stands where the pace-setters are as they swing into the enclosure, go over "the Chair" and the water hazard in front of the grandstand and swing hard left into the second lap. Now they are in sight again—what's left of them! Hardly a dozen remain of the twenty-seven that started. Two riderless horses are plunging along with the survivors. Somebody goes down at Becher's Brook. Here they come to the Canal Turn again. That isn't Pete Bostwick leading now. No, Pete is fourth or fifth, but fairly close to the leaders. He can pull it off yet. Three horses —Blue Prince, Reynoldstown, and Thomond II—come over the Canal Turn jump and go clumpity-clump for

GOLINKIN

BETWEEN PERIODS AT DELRAY

Valentine's. A gray is next—good old Uncle Batt, still sticking it. And right behind is Pete Bostwick on Castle Irwell, sailing over neatly as— A-a-a-ah! He's down! Pete's rolling along the turf like a shot rabbit. His horse stumbled slightly—just "pecked"—on landing but swerved sharply for the turn at the same time. They parted company. One minute riding for the grand prize, the next minute—bowling on the green! Pete stops rolling, rises, brushes himself off and looks up the course in time to see the riderless Castle Irwell disappear over the fence at Valentine's Brook. Pete shrugs his shoulders. Afoot in England! He starts walking. And that, for the Canal Turn onlookers, is the Grand National of 1935— except that word came down in a few minutes that Reynoldstown had won the race at odds of 22 to 1. It was an Irish jumper, Reynoldstown, and that night the Irish took Liverpool.

116

Now, it so happened that the little party from New York, via Chester, had ten shillings apiece on Reynoldstown because Dr. Shaun Hyde, M.F.H. of the Shaun Peel Hunt Club of Cork and brigade leader of the Irish clan at this Aintree meeting, was an old acquaintance of Guest Conductor Paul Brown and let him and his friends in on the good thing that was Reynoldstown. However, Paul Brown had English friends who were equally enthusiastic about other horses in the race and,

as a result, the Reynoldstown victory was not entirely a profit to the party. But it was a net profit and it further entitled the visitors from overseas to join the rejoicing Irish party in the streets and hotels of Liverpool that night.

The culmination came in the champagne dinner offer by Dr. Shaun Hyde himself, who had wagered a trifle on Reynoldstown himself and who, at the conclusion of the race, went into the paddock clinging to the tail of Frankie Furlong's winning dark brown gelding.

"For, mind you," said the M.F.H. of the Shaun Peel Hunt Club of Cork in a capacious private dining room in the Exchange Hotel, Liverpool, " 'twas the Duhallow

Hunt of Cork and the green turf of County Meath that won all the way today, and no mistake.''

There was, however, nothing on the race program to substantiate that statement.

Three O'Mearas and one Linehan rose in a protesting Corkonian chorus, but Dr. Shaun Hyde majestically waved them down as he took up the challenge.

"Is there no?" said Dr. Shaun. "Gregalach, Golden Miller, and Reynoldstown all foaled and bred within a couple of miles, as you might say. County Meath, no less. And well I know every foot of the turf they trod. Ireland f'r jumpers, me lad. That's the way of it. From away back, too. This Captain Becher of Becher's Brook—who was he? He's one of the Wrixon-Bechers, to be sure, the family that founded the Duhallow Hunt.'' (N.B. The good doctor pronounced it "Joohallow.") "That's the oldest hunt in Ireland and was founded in—in—what was it, Barry, me boy?''

"In 1772," said Whipper-in Barry O'Meara to the Master of the Shaun Peel hounds.

"In 1772 it was," said Dr. Hyde, going away again fast. "An' who belongs to the Duhallow Hunt by Major Noel Furlong, who owns Reynoldstown and—"

And lived in England, in Leicester. It was all in the papers.

"Do you tell me now?" said Dr. Shaun with a scornful laugh. "Well, he may live in Leicester or Timbuctoo; but he's Irish-bred like his horse, and so is Frankie, the grand lad. And haven't I seen them with me own eyes taking the banks with the Duhallow Hunt and half of Cork out there to enjiy the fun? There's where the boy —Frankie, I mean—learned to stick in the saddle the way he showed them today on Reynoldstown. Waiter, just give that magnum a bit of a tilt, d'ye see, and we'll have a health to the boy. And Jim, me lad, just scurry around a bit and see the boys started for the station. We must make the boat, ye know, f'r we've a p'int-to-p'int race to ride tomorrow, as well you know."

So Jim went off to scour the hotels to gather up the party that would be heading back to Cork and Dublin at midnight, and Dr. Shaun resumed:

"The way Frankie stuck on today—an' one very bad spot he had! He and Thomond came up to a jump together and Thomond swerved over on Reynoldstown as they jumped. I thought our lad was done for. He's down surely, I says to meself—but he wasn't. He came on all right, and I breathed again. And when we went into the paddock Frankie showed me what had happened. You know Willie Speck was riding Thomond. Well, when Thomond swerves over and comes bearin' into Reynolds-town at this jump, it's so close that Speck's heel comes down along the side of Frankie's britches and rips them to the boot-top. Clean as a whistle. Ah, well, it was that close but, sure, isn't it—"

"Tally-ho!" said Jim, standing in the doorway. "Party ready. Boat train waiting."

"We're off for Ireland," said Dr. Shaun Hyde, rising, glass in hand, "but we'll pause to drink once [sip] to Reynoldstown, once [sip] to the Furlongs, and once—bottoms up, me boys!—to the country that produces horses and men the like o' them!"

With which flourish the celebration ended, and the Grand National of 1935 became part of the history of horse racing.

To shift the scene back to the United States, anyone who knows anything about horses knows that the roots of the racing game are deep in the country soil and not

119

in the racing strips of Saratoga, Belmont Park, Arlington Park, Santa Anita or Hialeah. The backbone of racing as a sport is the long line of breeding farms in Virginia and Kentucky, the local horse shows of a hundred counties, the hunt clubs in the North and in the South, the amateur owners and riders, over timber and brush, the backers of the Upperville Horse Show, the Gold Cup

timber-jumping event at Warrenton, Virginia, the great Maryland Hunt Cup contest over timber jumps even higher than the buttressed brush fences at Aintree. From such ranks, and often by inheritance, come the millionaire owners of famous strings on the big-time turf. Flat racers or jumpers, show horses or mounts for the hunting field, hacks for families' riding—horses are horses to this great amateur clan, and not merely the implements of a great gambling game.

It must be admitted that the betting hordes at the big tracks are what keep that game flourishing in the style to which it is accustomed. But if the Whitneys, Wideners, Vanderbilts, and their aristocratic ilk quit the game cold and the horse-show, hunting-field, and hunt-meet clans turned to poultry farming or some other luxurious amusement, what was left of racing would

UPPERVILLE
COLT AND
HORSE SHOW

FIVE-GAITED CLASSES IN HAND

soon go downhill in a welter of chicanery and double-crossing. At Belmont Park one day a real racing follower by family tradition looked up from his newspaper and laughed. It was when the New York State Legislature was framing a mutuel bill "for the protection of the racing public."

"Protecting the bettors!" said the man who knew and loved racing as a sport. "Why, three out of every four bettors you see in line come out here with the intention of stealing everything they can lay their hands on!"

He might have added that millions who regularly bet on horse races never have been inside a race track and never have seen a race in their lives. And most of those who go to the track and bet day after day have no more sentimental interest in horses than they have in the little white ball in a spinning roulette wheel. It's money they're after, and they would see a fine thoroughbred run through a meat-chopper without blinking an eye if it meant an added two dollars in their pockets. The bettors maintain racing, but the horse lovers, the horse breeders, the horse showers, and the horse riders in the amateur field support it. If this support ever is withdrawn, there will be nothing above to maintain. The garish super-structure will crash, and the bettors will go back to their dice, their cards, their roulette wheels, and their "numbers games," which is their proper field, anyway.

But a real follower of the turf, one who knows horses and looks on the game as a sport, can find outlet for his enthusiasm at the Upperville Horse Show in rural Virginia as well as at Belmont Park on Futurity Day. Upperville is mentioned merely because it is perhaps the oldest horse show in the country, though it doesn't pretend to rival THE Horse Show in Madison Square Garden

122

in New York for entries, for swank or for total attendance. In fact, the annual Upperville gathering is more of a colt show than a horse show, and it was with colts that it started a few years before the Civil War. It seems that local owners of rival colts appealed to Colonel Richard Hunter Dulany, a good judge of horses, to settle a dispute as to which of their two colts was the better. Colonel Dulany demurred but finally was induced to appoint a day for the judging. Virginians being naturally interested in horses, a crowd gathered for the ceremony, and, if history has it right, that was the beginning of the horse-show sport and business (combining the best features of both) in this country. Except for two years of the Civil War, the Upperville show has been held annually ever since.

Another part of the program that followers of racing as a sport can enjoy is the annual sale of yearlings during the Saratoga season. There in the big pavilion across the road from the main track the yearlings of famous breeding lines are led in at night and knocked down to the highest bidders. Sometimes, if the weather is very warm, the selling takes place outside under the elms and maples. But generally the ceremony goes on in the pavilion. There's a stage at one end for the auctioneer and his assistants. In front of the stage is a roped-off square that looks something like a prize ring. Stretching back through the pavilion, which is open on three sides, are about five hundred camp chairs. These chairs are occupied by the same crowd whose names you may read on the box holders' list in the Metropolitan Opera program. Many of the bidders are in evening clothes.

There a yearling may be knocked down for anything from $100—that was the minimum as ruled by the late

Ed Tranter, who wielded the gavel for many years—to $75,000, which was the top price the last time this observer looked over the sales slips. The $75,000 purchase was a yearling named New Broom, and, sad to say, it didn't amount to anything in particular on the track. But Flying Ebony, bred by John E. Madden, was sold as a yearling there to Gifford Cochran at a much more reasonable sum and went on to win the Kentucky Derby. Preakness and Futurity winners came out of that same pavilion, bid in by a lucky nod of the head or the lifting of a significant finger while the auctioneer's hammer was raised on a summer's night.

But mention of Saratoga recalls the great meeting between Gallant Fox, the Belair Stud star, and Whichone, the pick of the H. P. Whitney string, in what turned out to be a jim-dandy affair. That was back in 1930, and the natives still chuckle when they recall it. The race was the historic Travers, which traces back to the Civil War era. Franklin D. Roosevelt, then Governor of New York, was on hand for the gala occasion. Gallant Fox was the winner of the Preakness, the Derby, and the Belmont. Whichone was the idol of the H. P. Whitney stables. The great Earl Sande, the Singing Kid from Deep River, was to ride Gallant Fox. Sonny Workman, chunky and pugnacious, who would grit his teeth and ride a horse through a knothole if it was the only way to win, was to have the leg up on Whichone. As for owners, it was the Harry Payne Whitney of ancient, affluent, and honorable lineage against William Woodward, a banker, the president of the Jockey Club and, according to the ladies, the handsomest figure in racing for all his gray hairs. There were four entries for the Travers, but nobody bothered about the other two. All the talk was of Gallant Fox and Whichone. It was to be a two-horse race, and a great one.

Through the night before the race the Whichone supporters were worrying about track conditions. It was raining. A sticky track would handicap their equine idol. They sat up late, hoping to see the rain cease. They were up at dawn. Gray skies, but the rain had stopped. At seven A.M. the sun broke through the clouds, and Whichone's stock went up several points. Like Napoleon looking over the field of battle before giving orders to his cavalry leader, the tall and handsome Mr. Woodward appeared on the clubhouse porch at ten o'clock and surveyed the track. He nodded and walked away. Almost any kind of track would suit him. Gallant Fox had gone unbeaten through a great season, rain or shine. In the Travers there was nothing to worry about except Whichone, and the Whitney thoroughbred's chances hadn't been helped by the rain of the previous night. So Mr. Woodward nodded quietly and walked away. He was satisfied—and even confident.

Shortly after midday a heavy shower came up. The rain came spilling down fast, but not any faster than the tears coursed down the cheeks of the Whitney-Whichone supporters. Trainer Tom Healey of the Whitney string sat on the porch of his cottage, just across from Whichone's stall at the Whitney stable beyond the backstretch of the main track, and said never a word. Perhaps he was speechless from grief. Whichone wore bar plates, and, in sticky going, mud balls up under bar plates in a way to annoy a horse no little when the main idea is to turn on full speed. Around the track and through the town there was a dread that Whichone would be scratched because of the weather. It would be fair enough, as racing strategy, but it would spoil the great event. It would be no contest. As the half-hours passed and there was no official notice that Whichone had been scratched, hope arose again. The great race was still on.

The Whitney clan and the Whichone handlers were sure their thoroughbred was a better animal than "that big white-eyed horse" called Gallant Fox that the veteran trainer, Sunny Jim Fitzsimmons, would be bringing over from the farthest stable out on the "Oklahoma" training sector across Union Avenue from the main track. Whichone was beaten in the Belmont, but the Travers would bring revenge! When the midday shower spent itself and the sun came out again, they were sure of a Whitney victory. They figured that Whichone would hold the Fox to the upper turn and then outfoot him in the stretch drive. So the piebald lead pony was made ready, and Whichone was blanketed, with confidence, for the big event.

In the interim a colorful crowd had been pouring into the Saratoga stands, jamming every quarter and overflowing into the shrubbery around. There were rich racing followers who had come thousands of miles to see the Travers. There were summer visitors at the Spa who ordinarily wouldn't have known one horse from another at a race track, but they had heard of Gallant Fox and Whichone and were out to see the fun. The earlier races passed almost unheeded. The sole—and ungrammatical—question passing around was: "Who do you like in the big race?"

Finally there was a shout from some sharp-eyed scouts. They had sighted the pinto pony that led the Whitney horses to the races. It was coming around the lane at the

lower turn of the track, with a darker animal being led behind. That would be Whichone. There was a rush for the paddock, where the rivals would be saddled under separate trees.

Gallant Fox, a glowing chestnut, already was there surrounded by an admiring throng. Earl Sande, probably the greatest of modern jockeys, was standing near by wearing the Belair Stud silks. His arms were folded, and he was talking quietly with the stout, venerable, and amiable "Sunny Jim" Fitzsimmons, trainer of the Belair string. The Whitney supporters gathered around Whichone under a neighboring tree. A little way off two other horses were being made ready for the race, Jim Dandy, owned by Chaffee Earl, and Sun Falcon, owned by Willis Sharpe Kilmer, but nobody paid any attention to those horses. That is, nobody except the handlers thereof and maybe a few kind friends.

The bugler blew "Jockeys up!" and the crowd in the paddock scattered and made for the grandstand as the jockeys walked their horses out through the gate to the track. With only four starters, there was little delay at the barrier. Suddenly there was a roar from the crowd. The race was on. It was Sonny Workman who had the rail with Whichone and, as they flashed past the clubhouse, he had a lead of a neck over Gallant Fox. They swung that way around the lower turn and went up the backstretch almost like a team with the "off horse" lagging a trifle. Workman was watching his famous rival, Sande. Sonny had his head turned so that he was actually staring Gallant Fox in the face. But it was Sande he was watching. The other horses? They were nowhere. A man with his glasses fixed on Whichone and Gallant Fox didn't even get the two trailers in his field of vision. Who cared about them, anyway? On up the backstretch the

130

great rivals pounded, holding the same relative posi-
tions. They swung around the upper turn and then,
while the cries still were "Come on, Workman!" or
"Sande! Sande! Sande!" it was noticed through the
glasses that another horse had come into the field of
vision. And it was coming fast.

Into the stretch they turned and, to the horror of
thousands, the third horse came on—and on—and—well,
it simply ran over the two stars of the turf. Gallant Fox
and Whichone, in their furious rivalry, had run each
other breathless, and Jim Dandy, at 50 to 1, 100 to 1, or
150 to 1, as luck would have it—"Write your own ticket,"
said the bookies laughingly—was an easy winner. Whichone broke down in the last quarter and, pulling up as
quickly as he could after going under the wire, Workman jumped to the ground and led his disabled thoroughbred back to the weighing-in stand.

So that was the great race that had packed the Spa and
filled the Saratoga stands to overflowing, the heralded
meeting of Gallant Fox, with a string of victories that
included the Kentucky Derby, the Preakness, and the
Belmont, and Whichone, the star of the Whitney stable.
It was a great race between them to the head of the
stretch—and it had a Jim Dandy finish.

"I know that Jim Dandy," said a stout and irate
gentleman as he signaled for his limousine at the clubhouse portico. "He did that same thing last year in the
Grand Union Hotel Stakes!"

The irate gentleman seemed to imply such things were
an absolute outrage and should be prevented by law.

One day at the Empire City there bobbed up a book
reviewer who had a volume of Tennyson in his pocket.
The Pinkertons are supposed to watch out for suspicious

HACKNEYS

characters of all sorts, but they must not have been on the alert that day. So the book reviewer came in un-molested and joined a group of trainers seated on the steps of the clubhouse porch, a cool spot. Tom Healey was there and so was Derby Dick Thompson, head trainer of the E. R. Bradley string. The second race was coming up. Derby Dick had just come from saddling one of the Bradley horses and sending it off toward the barrier. Bien Joli was the name of the horse. The name of a Bradley horse must start with a B, of course. In answer to the query of a bystander, Derby Dick said quietly that he liked his horse's chance in the race.

"And what horse," said the same bystander to the book reviewer who was browsing there, "do you like in this race?"

"Why, I hadn't even looked at the card," said the book reviewer. "Let's see."

He pulled a program from his pocket, looked at the second race entries and said:

"I like Tintagel. I hope he wins."

"So do a lot of others," said the heckler. "But why do you pick him? Inside information?"

"Yes, inside this book," said the book reviewer, bringing the limp volume of Tennyson out of his pocket. "Tintagel is the only name on the card that means anything to me. Ever read about King Arthur and the Knights of the Round Table in 'Idylls of the King'? King Arthur was born in the castle of Tintagel, according to the legend. Look here."

He opened the book to page 9 and quoted:

> *"The prince and warrior, Gorloïs, he that held*
> *Tintagil Castle by the Cornish sea."*

"H'm-m-m!" said the heckler, looking down at his program again. "It's a Marshall Field colt and an odds-on favorite. That tip from Tennyson isn't so hot."

"Well, look!" said the book reviewer who had shelved his volume and pulled out his program again. "Here's more Arthurian dope. Tintagel was sired by Sir Gallahad III. But that Gallahad is spelled wrong. How did they get that extra *l* in there?"

Mr. Clem McCarthy, who knows all, sees all, and tells all about horses, happened along just in time to hear that query and pop back quickly with an answer.

"Why, because it was written that way for the racing register by a man who knew more about horses than poetry," said Mr. McCarthy briskly. "But don't let a little thing like that worry you. I know a better one still. It's a classic."

"Well," said Derby Dick Thompson, looking up from his seat on the steps, "Captain Cassatt had a horse named Garbage, but maybe that ain't classic."

"The one I mean," said Mr. McCarthy, "was a horse named Alcibiades that ran in the Derby some years ago."

"A good name," said the book reviewer mildly. "What was the matter? Did they spell it wrong?"

"Oh, no! The spelling was perfect," said Mr. McCarthy with a grin, "but this Alcibiades was a filly!"

"Suffering Plutarch!" said the book reviewer, backing away in horror. "That was a regular rasper!"

"There was a horse running at Saratoga a few years ago," said the original heckler, cutting in, "and his name was Woinomoinen. I thought that was a queer one, so I asked how come. Well, they told me the trainer had a little daughter—just a toddler—and the morning the colt is born he comes back to the house, wondering what name to give to the colt. While he's talking to his wife about it, the little girl, who's looking out the window, turns around and says, 'Woino moinen, Daddy,' meaning it's a rainy morning. And that's what they called the colt."

"A very pretty story," said the book reviewer.

"A triple-dashed piece of tripe!" said the heckler. "I found out later that Woinomoinen was one of the great heroes of Danish legend. That's where the name came from."

"And how did you learn it?" asked the book reviewer, turning a suspicious look on the race-track regular.

"I read it in George Borrow's 'Lavengro,' " said the heckler sheepishly.

"Let that be a lesson to you!" said the book reviewer severely.

"Speaking of names," said Derby Dick Thompson, "there was a big owner—I won't mention his name; he's dead now, anyway. He had a horse in the Derby. Just a few hours before post time for the Derby, Colonel Matt Winn got a call from town. They had this owner in jail."

"Hadn't paid his feed bill?"

"It wasn't feed—it was drink," said Derby Dick. "It was in Prohibition days. Somebody invited him into a private car, and the enforcement agents busted in while he had the bottle at his lips. He told them who he was, but they didn't believe him. Anybody could say he owned a horse that was starting in the Derby. But finally they let him phone Matt Winn and, of course, Matt got him out. No, his horse didn't win. The story isn't that good. But it's good enough. Do you know what that horse's name was?"

"No," said the book reviewer.

"Revenue Agent," said Derby Dick with a grin.

At that moment Mr. McCarthy barked, "They're off!" and everybody looked across the track to where the field in the second race was scurrying away from the starting gate. They whirled around the upper turn and pounded down in front of the grandstand, pulling up as they passed the group on the clubhouse steps. The winner: Tintagel!

"Hey!" said the original heckler, turning suddenly on the book reviewer. "Look in that book of yours and see what Tennyson has for the third race."

There are many strange stories of the turf, including the story of a horse called Chase Me, the pride of Maryland, a gorgeous gelding with an astonishing career that culminated in a meeting with the great Equipoise in the Metropolitan Handicap of 1934 at Belmont Park, which neither horse won.

Some years before that, the late Uncle Wilbert Robinson of baseball fame, who lived in Baltimore, was arranging for a fishing party on Chesapeake Bay.

"We're going out with Cliff Bosley," bellowed the large round Robbie in his greathearted way. "Now listen, you outlanders. Maybe you never heard of Cliff Bosley; but he's a grand feller, and I'll tell you why. All the Bosleys are grand. If you meet any one around Maryland by the name of Bosley, you're meeting the best there is. Never forget that."

Uncle Wilbert's blast to the visiting fishermen was recalled when Chase Me rose to sudden fame on the turf. Now, whether the Bosley children who fed, petted, and rode a family hunter named Chase Me were kin to Uncle Wilbert's seagoing Bosley or not, Maryland agreed with the Robinson statement as a whole. The Bosleys belonged with the best people. And these Bosleys had a fine hunter and show horse in Chase Me. It was Mrs.

THE MOUNTIES

Elizabeth Bosley's favorite horse, but it also was a play-mate of the children. It did any number of tricks. When it first was sent to a starting gate on the track, an assistant starter walked up to the gelding to grab the reins and lead it into the right stall. Chase Me, seeing a stranger approach, gravely lifted the right front paw for a hand-shake.

But there was no thought of taking the fine show horse and jumper into the racing game until one day when Mrs. Bosley wanted to give one of her flat runners a workout. Chase Me was drafted into service as a pace-setter, just a companion to encourage the real racer to get going and keep going. To the astonishment of Mrs. Bosley and all involved, the show horse, the good hunter, the family pet, simply ran away from the flat runner. If the gelding was that fast, why not send it to the races? After all, it was worth a trial—and Chase Me was sired by the great Purchase. So a trial was decided upon. It certainly was a novel experiment. Flat runners are often turned into good steeplechasers or fine hunters. But no one recalled any hunter or show horse that had turned to flat racing and gained anything thereby.

Nevertheless, Chase Me went to the races from the hunting field and the show ring. A good little jockey, Duke Bellizzi, had the leg up on the handsome gelding in its first start, which was at Havre de Grace. Chase Me won. And won again and again. Seven victories in a row, including one over Mate, a Preakness winner and one of the good stake horses of the day. The success of the former hunter was sensational. Seven starts, seven vic-tories—and this on the big-time turf by a horse that had wandered in from the hunting field, and was a show horse and a family pet that did tricks into the bargain.

137

Possibly the amazing gelding could beat even the great Equipoise, the "big horse" of that racing era. That was the talk, and that was the situation as they both went to the barrier for the Metropolitan Handicap at Belmont of a fine spring day in 1934.

Equipoise had won the Metropolitan twice in a row and was out to make it three straight. Under such circumstances, Mrs. Bosley wanted the best rider she could get for Chase Me, the sensation of the turf, the pride of Maryland and the Bosley family pet. She engaged Mack Garner, one of the coolest and best, a veteran who, shortly before that, had ridden Cavalcade through the twilight to a Derby victory in old Kentucky. But, at the last moment, it was discovered that Mack Garner wouldn't ride. Why not? Well, Mack was a regular rider for the Brookmeade Stable, and no riders of the Brookmeade Stable would ride that day. They were in mourning. One of their stablemates had gone down off Psychic Bid, had been trampled by steel-shod hoofs—and was to be buried on the day of the Metropolitan Handicap. That dead jockey was Duke Bellizzi, the boy who had ridden Chase Me to his first victory on the turf. That was why Mack Garner wouldn't ride and why another boy, a steeplechase jockey hastily recruited, was hoisted into the saddle.

And perhaps that was the reason that the horse followed the jockey. Because on the day that Duke Bellizzi was buried—the little Duke who had ridden Chase Me to that flying start on a sensational career—Chase Me was buried, too. It was, in a tragic way, in keeping with the whole astonishing episode that was the gelding's great rush to glory—and death—on the turf. Here was a horse that had gone blithely over the stiffest post-and-

138

rail courses in the Maryland hunt meets, that had galloped unhurt over hill and dale and strange fences and ditches behind the hounds. But on this day at Belmont, running against the brilliant Equipoise and others on a flat track, confronted by no fences or ditches, running free of interference, Chase Me's legs crossed; down went the horse, one leg broken. Seven starts, seven victories; an eighth start—victory or death—it was death.

Equipoise finished first but was disqualified for interference, which was a shock to the racing gentry, but not such a shock as the sudden end to the racing career of the great gelding from the hunting fields. Racing folk are superstitious. They still tell the tale of Chase Me—of how Duke Bellizzi rode the horse to its first victory, how Bellizzi died; how the jockey to ride Chase Me was changed for that reason; how Bellizzi was buried that Saturday and—well, the horse followed the jockey; that's all.

[Quotation from Henri Murger's "Scènes de la Vie de Bohème": "Premier Lecteur: 'Je le disais bien; ce n'était pas gai, cette histoire.' Que voulez-vous, lecteur? On ne peut pas toujours rire!"]

There remain the harness hosses (preferred spelling) to be considered. There is confessed a fondness here for the harness hosses ever since—far away and long ago—youthful hours were spent in Dutchess County, New York, twilights guarding a slim chestnut mare, Varvana (2:24 1/4), home from the Grand Circuit and cropping the grass in a rich meadow as the dusk deepened, the brook near by babbling a running accompaniment to the reiterated chant of a whippoorwill—its head plainly bobbing with each throbbing call—perched lengthwise

139

on a fence rail not ten yards away. And since then there have been trips to the Land o' Goshen where the great Hambletonian is run each year, where the trotters and pacers were in full force, where truly rural rooters, one and all, knew the nigh-side from the off-side of a hoss, where fried chicken and sweet corn were served in the big refreshment tent, where the old auction pools were sold "viva voce" by the vastly entertaining gaffers who were eventually coldly overthrown by the "iron men," the mutuel machines. *Eheu, fugaces!*

There trotted such notable and noble animals as the great Greyhound, Lord Jim, the Marchioness—and who could say how many from the Hanover barns? There was the old excitement of the "scoring" for the start, the shrewd maneuvers of the veterans in the bucket-seats of their almost-gossamer sulkies, the flourishing of whips, the slapping of reins, the patter of hoofs and the "Har! Har!" of the drivers as they whirled off leaving a cloud of rising dust in their wake.

On the general subject of harness hosses there once arrived a letter, the contents of which are herewith exposed to view:

Sir:

I can't speak for you folks from York State, but the real old homestead of the trottin' hoss was in New England and the rise of the harness hoss in a sportin' way is due to the natural piety of the Pilgrim Fathers and their subsequent descendants. Of which I am one.

Now, we didn't hold much with trottin' matches as such, you understand. (Oh, by the way, Oliver Wendell Holmes long ago warned against referring to a "trottin' race"—it's always a trottin' match to those who know anything about harness hosses.) No, we didn't set out to make a public spectacle and bring around

bettors and riffraff and all that, but we did like to drive a nice-steppin' hoss to meetin' come Sunday, you know. I wouldn't wonder if the best Morgans, Todds and Wilkes trottin' hosses in New England in recent years inherit their trottin' proclivities from sires and dams bred for the express purpose of taking folks to church on Sundays, some goin' a leetle—just a leetle—faster'n others, of course.

Mention of the Hambletonian brings me memories of trots and paces on the old short ship circuit in and near the Connecticut Valley, of farmers who hurried their milkin' in order to match hosses on the nearest half-mile track—or even just a good stretch of village road, probably called the Pike—after supper. Supper, mind you. Not dinner. This is New England, where we eat dinner at dinnertime, which is noon, and if we like pie for breakfast, we eat pie for breakfast, and there is no butler about by the name of Jeeves to gasp at the barbarism and bust the buttons off 'is livery in stark 'orror.

Yes, sir, off would go the farmers after supper and have a brush with their hosses with mebbe as much as ten bushel of oats at stake. It's pretty late for me to be tellin' tales out o' school, but when I was a boy I heard tell of other boys—I said other boys—my father is still hale and hearty and has strict ideas about the wuth of schoolin' to a youngster—who went off and wickedly played hookey in order to see the trottin' matches at the nearest driving park. You could get in without public notice by climbing an elm tree, creeping out on a branch and dropping down over the fence. The track is still there and the elm tree, too. I could give the exact location, but I don't wish to encourage such sinful goings-on among youngsters.

Well, sir, the greatest little mare that ever lived—to many who saw that race about thirty years ago at Northampton—was Princess Wilkes, a weasel-bellied roan mare with short legs and a natural pacer of the Roan Wilkes strain. Morgans, I believe. The Wilkes mare paced without a checkrein, her neck stretched out like a runnin' hoss, and nobody ever saw her break. She wore no hopples, no fancy straps. She raced clean and she went fast. We wintered her, one year, and come time for training, I had

142

my great thrill. She was hitched to a gig and the genial driver said to me in the stable yard: "Son, you wanter take her fer a spin 'round the track?" Me!

Now, I guess that wasn't the fastest mile that ever was paced. Since that time I've flown in a plane that was making four miles a minute. But, somehow, I still feel that the fastest ride I ever had in my life was in that rattling gig on the old half-mile track when I held the reins—all alone, by gosh!—on the great Princess Wilkes. But there was serious work ahead. Aconite, a bay gelding and a Grand Circuit winner, had to be beat. Billy Crozier drove the Wilkes mare. Tarnation take it! Aconite won in four heats. As a pious Yankee—there are generations of deacons in my family—I bow to the mysterious ways of Providence; but the victory of Aconite was a great strain on my religious convictions. I did think that right and justice demanded a triumph for Princess Wilkes, so the best conclusion I could come to was that the Lord couldn't have been looking and the Devil pulled a nasty trick that day. But the Wilkes mare, in winning one heat, paced the fastest mile ever made on that track—2:11 and a fraction—which was some satisfaction.

I'm not a licensed historian, and mebbe it's just a legend of New England; but the elders up my way in Massachusetts used to say that Governor Channing Cox of the sovereign State of Massachusetts, a Harvard graduate and a mighty fine lawyer, used to get as much credit for being the brother of Walter Cox, the famous Grand Circuit driver, as he did for being the Chief Executive of the Commonwealth. Some folks had it that Walter's earnings with the harness hosses helped Channing through college. I wouldn't know about that, but if it's true it reflects credit on all concerned, including the trottin' hosses.

There's another story they tell up my way, and some even say it was one of the deacons in my own family that gave the caution to his boys as they were settin' off for the county fair. "Don't you boys be a-bettin' on the trottin' matches," hollered the deacon as the boys were starting out in the buggy. Then he hollered a mite louder: "We don't hold with gamblin' in any shape or form— remember that!" And just as the gig turned at the gate into the

143

main road he hollered loudest of all: "But ef you must bet, put your money on Hodge's gray mare!"

Times have changed, and the old Holmes (Oliver Wendell) ain't considered what he used to be; but he liked a good trottin' hoss, and he was a man of good standing in New England. Yes, sir, the mild Autocrat knew hosses and loved 'em and wrote about 'em, and just for a sample I would like to bring your attention to one section of a poem he wrote entitled: "Man Wants But Little Here Below," the section being as follows:

> *I would not have the horse I drive*
> *So fast that folks must stop and stare;*
> *An easy gait—two, forty-five—*
> *Suits me; I do not care—*
> *Perhaps, for just a single spurt,*
> *Some seconds less would do no hurt.*

Well, sir, that's the real old New England sperrit and I wouldn't have it otherwise. Good men like good hosses. I'll say no more at present except that our folks are well but it's been terrible dry this summer and the Baldwins and Newtown pippins are just a lot of nubbins this year.

Yours in double harness,

(Signed)   JONATHAN EDWARDS THE YOUNGER.

That missive carries the full flavor of the New England attitude toward the harness hosses and, with regard to local authorities, it might be mentioned—as it was by Oliver Wendell Holmes himself—that once when the Autocrat made a slight error in giving the time record for a mile by the famous Lady Suffolk, it was none other than Ralph Waldo Emerson who checked him gently and set him right. So, go to Goshen with a clear conscience on Hambletonian Day. Enjoy the truly rural surroundings, the fields of tall corn almost ready for the short-bladed cutter, the haycocks in the meadows, the apple trees burdened down with ripening fruit, the gay crowd at the Good Time track, the whirling panorama of the Hambletonian itself: a Peter Scott winning in straight heats, driven by the veteran Fred Egan, beating the giant Remus (over 17 hands), Kuno and six more pursuers—that was the Hambletonian of 1940. And, going home in the twilight, take some proper pride in the feeling that at least one heritage has not been wasted, and that the harness hosses of the United States, now as in the past, are the fastest and finest in the world.

MILITARY JUMPING

145

SERMONS IN STONES

(About 4 down to Rudyard Kipling)

When I was a handicap golfer—verging a bit on the wild—
I gathered my weapons for battle, gladsome and gay as a child.
My woods had been singing and soaring; my irons were crisp
   to the pin;
So I teed up this day in the tourney and felt in my heart I
   would win.

Long from the tee through the fairway, clearing all briar and
   fern,
Headed for triumph and glory, two under 4's to the turn;
Sudden I sliced to a gully; there I saw carved on a stone:
"After me cometh a golfer. Tell him I, too, have known."

Laughed as I swung with my niblick; but who can contend with
   his fate?
The 7 I took was a prelude to the next where I garnered an 8!
Black was my soul at the searing; white were my lips with the
   curse;
Broken and weary and wilted, I stumbled from horror to worse.

Cornered at last in a quarry, fronting a huge granite mass,
Broke all my clubs in a fury, scattered my card on the grass.
Only I sent for a chisel—only I carved on a stone:
"After me cometh a golfer. Tell him I, too, have known!"

146

IT WAS a distressingly hot day, and hardly a breath of air was stirring. Flies were buzzing around the superheated courtroom. The magistrate leaned forward and said to the prisoner at the bar, a mild-appearing gent enough:

"Why did you shoot him?"

The prisoner at the bar told a rambling tale. He was called to order a dozen times by the magistrate and four times by his own counsel; but he blundered ahead, and the whole miserable story came out. He had gone out to his golf club that day, as was his custom. He was small of stature, as any one could see. He was a peaceful man by instinct and habit. The automatic pistol? Well, he carried that because he was erratic off the tee—usually landed in the underbrush, often down some ravine—and he was afraid of snakes. There were a lot of snakes lurking in the underbrush out there. He could get plenty of players to prove that. When they sliced into the brush you could hear them hacking and whacking around in there, and when the ball bounded out on the fairway again they were "playing 3"; and the noise was due to killing a snake in there, or maybe a couple of snakes. It was a common occurrence.

Well, he was playing with this fellow Smirk in the club tournament for Class D players. He never had liked this Smirk, anyway. He referred to Mr. Smirk once as "the deceased." The magistrate looked at the police sergeant in surprise, and the police sergeant glared savagely at the mumbling prisoner. He, the prisoner, had taken three putts on the first green. It was annoying, but it was a habit with him and he bore up under it. This Smirk, "the deceased," who had taken only one putt but was still three feet from the hole, conceded himself that putt to win the hole 6-5. He asked Smirk not

147

to do that. He thought all putts should be holed out. It was in the rules. Smirk—"the deceased"—was a big, pot-bellied man and he had a loud, overbearing laugh. He used it a lot. Too much. He laughed when the prisoner said a man ought to hole out his putts.

The prisoner reminded this Smirk of what once happened at the Winged Foot Golf Club when the late and lamented "Nibs" Nobles was the president. It was about the time that Bob Jones slaughtered Al Espinosa in the play-off for the open championship there. In 1929—that was right, thank you, Judge. It seems that, in a club tournament, one man conceded himself a three-foot putt on the first green. His opponent thereupon conceded himself a ten-footer on the second green. The first offender then conceded himself a full brassie shot to the green at the third, whereupon the party of the second part pulled a masterly trick. After slicing into the rough off the fourth tee, he conceded himself the match by 5 up and 4 to play. The matter was carried to the club president, "Nibs" Nobles, who took proper action. He had both offenders driven off the club grounds with sticks and their names stricken from the rolls.

So the conceding of putts led to trouble, as the prisoner had told "the deceased," and he said it over again at the second green where this fellow Smirk conceded himself another annoying putt. But the real argument began at the third green. The prisoner said to Smirk:

"If you're so sure of holing it, why don't you hole it?"

"Why, it's ridiculous to waste the time," said Smirk. "Nobody could miss a putt like that."

"Not if he picked up without trying," agreed the defendant; "but I once saw Walter Hagen miss one like that—and Macdonald Smith miss one shorter."

148

Smirk roared with laughter and smote the defendant on the back, making him cough. When the coughing spell was over, the defendant said to Smirk:

"I warn you against conceding yourself another putt of any kind."

At the fourth green Smirk had a three-footer, and the prisoner at the bar glared at him so fiercely that he decided to hole it out. To his discomfiture, the ball rolled by the hole—but not far, because this Smirk reached out with his putter while it was still rolling and hooked it back. It's an old trick. It makes it impossible to miss the next one, there being no next one to miss. In addition to being an old trick on the links, it was the last straw in this case. The defendant, at this point, admitted drawing his automatic and dropping this Smirk in his tracks.

He didn't remember much of what happened after that. He came in and told some fellows around the club about it. The police had come. The automatic was on the table right there. Only one shot had been fired. Rules were rules. If those fellows who conceded themselves putts think they couldn't miss 'em, why do they go on for years refusing to hole 'em? He had no feeling of regret. He was not sorry for Mr. Smirk, "the deceased."

"Why do you call him the deceased?" queried the magistrate.

"What!" said the little prisoner with a wild look. "Isn't he dead?"

"No, no!" said the magistrate. "Nothing as bad as that. Just a light flesh wound. He's in the corridor, and we'll have him right in to testify. You're lucky it's for felonious assault and not first-degree murder."

150

The little man seemed stunned for a moment. Then he jumped up, grabbed the automatic off the table, and dashed into the corridor. Two shots were heard. The little man came back into the courtroom, tossed the automatic back on the table, and said with an air of deep satisfaction:

"Okay now. Make it murder."

And thus the case was brought to a successful conclusion and the story has a happy ending.

Please note the gallant golfer as from tee to green he hies;
For fun (or doctor's orders) he is taking exercise.
His head he carries (rather high), one club (that made the stroke).
He also carries matches just in case he wants a smoke.
And with the gallant golfer, as he wanders west and east,
There trudges forth a skinny kid who's burdened like a beast.
The lad who seeks no exercise but just his caddie fees,
Goes carting total tonnage that would spring a pack-mule's knees.
The golfer gay who goes his way a-whacking at the ball
May have the fun. But exercise? The caddie gets it all!

Of course, championship golf is different. It's a deadly serious matter. The nervous strain is terrific at times. Even the greatest of them all, the Emperor Jones, was known to have become violently nauseated after reaching the clubhouse with another championship added to his glittering string. Some fellows showed it in other ways. Some didn't show it at all. But they felt it just the same.

After Bob Jones retired from competition, the best of the young amateurs was the chesty and chunky W. Lawson Little, Jr., a long hitter, a very deliberate player, and rather a moody chap. In 1934 he won the British amateur championship and the United States amateur championship. In 1935 he won the British amateur championship again, and in September he was at the Country Club of Cleveland to make it a "double double" if he could, British and United States amateur champion two years in a row. No previous amateur golfer—not even Robert Tyre Jones, Jr., of Atlanta, Georgia—had been able to do that.

By the time he had completed the fourth round over the Country Club course at Cleveland, Lawson had won twenty-seven consecutive matches in championship play here and abroad. With the hazards of match play and the fact that many of these encounters were at eighteen holes, this was an extraordinary and unprecedented demonstration of positive superiority in a field. But he had some narrow escapes, and the pressure was on all the way. In the fifth round at Cleveland he came to the fifth hole 1 down. The hole is a short one—about 200 yards—a shot from an elevated tee to a green below with trees at the rear. Those spectators lingering around the fifth tee knew it was Lawson Little coming up because of the thundering herd that moved with the match, rushing to the ropes that blocked off the fairway and clustering six-deep in a circle around the green. Only Lawson drew such galleries at amateur golf tournaments since Bob Jones had become a galleryite himself.

The fifth tee is in something of a leafy nook on that course. Elms, maples, and beech trees formed a backdrop for the scene as the marshals cleared a path for two players to step out on the tee. One was Lawson Little in gray knickers and a white shirt open at the throat. The other was W. B. (Duff) McCullough of Philadelphia, a well built young fellow. He was wearing long trousers and a yellow shirt with the sleeves rolled up. A pretty good golfer, this McCullough. He might beat anybody in the world at eighteen holes—and this was one of the eighteen-hole rounds of the championship.

McCullough was 1 up. He had slapped an approach shot dead to the pin at the third hole. That was how he became 1 up. There was a hush around the tee on the heights and around the fifth green below when Mc-Cullough teed up his ball and studied his shot to the green. There were traps in front of the green and maple trees just over the back corners. Lawson Little was standing back against the ropes, watching McCullough. He looked a bit tired, though it was still the forenoon of a bright September day. But twenty-seven victories in a row. Three championships behind him. Every time he teed up at Cleveland he was faced by a stranger who began tossing birdies at him. It was the chance of a life-time for each of these strangers. They might knock off the great Lawson Little and leap from obscurity to inter-national notice. If Lawson hadn't been keen—and lucky —he would have been out of this tournament before he ever met McCullough.

And this McCullough now. Looked like a good golfer. Must have been good to get to the fifth round. Lawson had played par golf over the first four holes and he was 1 down. This McCullough had pulled himself out of two horribly tight spots the day before to beat Jack West-land, a Walker Cup player and a former finalist in the amateur championship, runner-up to Francis Ouimet at Beverly Hills, Chicago, in 1931. It stood to reason that McCullough would be no cinch, especially at eighteen holes.

McCullough hit the ball. Lawson watched it sail straight out, curve a bit to the left, and drop on the green with a little roll that left it fifteen feet from the pin. A good shot. It gave Lawson something to think about. He was 1 down, and this fellow was on the green with a fair chance for a 2. They were right when they said this bird from Philadelphia was tough.

Lawson teed up his ball. He didn't like the spot he had chosen. He bent over, picked up the ball, and teed up again a yard away. Maybe he was worrying too much. Would it be so terrible if he lost a golf match? It was only a game. His life didn't go with it. What would happen if he turned around to the crowd at the tee and said: "I'm fed up with this, and I'm going back to the hotel and have a good long sleep"? Suppose he dubbed his shot—just spilled it off the tee. Any other golfer could do that, and no questions asked. But the triple winner of British and United States amateur crowns didn't have that privilege. Why should good work bring a consequent burden? Somehow there was something all wrong with the whole thing. It was tiresome and silly. Then Lawson hit the ball.

It sailed out across the little valley. Lawson's club was still held high over his head. The ball dropped just beyond the pin, bit into the green carpet and rolled about fifteen feet beyond. The gallery burst into tremendous applause. The British and United States amateur champion was living up to his reputation. Those who had bought tickets to see him were getting the worth of their money. This McCullough now. Just a pretty good golfer. But watch Lawson Little cut him down. Those other fellows blow hot and cold, but a real champion works grimly away and gets 'em in the end. See the cool way

Lawson had hit that one? Another fellow might have been jarred by McCullough's pretty shot—and McCullough already 1 up. But it only spurred Little to doing better. That's why he was a champion. He came through under pressure.

The players, with a mob swirling down the hillside in their wake, went on to the green. There was a question as to which was away. The distances were measured with the flagstick. McCullough was away. It was his putt. He sighted it carefully. Lawson leaned on his putter at the back edge of the green and watched. Probably that fellow would knock the ball right into the cup. They were always pulling things like that on him—especially on the first nine. Too bad he couldn't start his matches on the tenth. The first nine at Cleveland had been a nightmare to him.

Duff McCullough stroked his ball smoothly toward the hole, but it was a bad putt. He was short—about sixteen inches short of the cup. He should have been up, at least. Here was a chance for the champion to show that fellow something. Roll this in, and Mr. McCullough from Philadelphia would realize that there were reasons why a man won three big amateur championships in a row.

Lawson looked over his line of putt. He liked it. No "borrow" to figure either way. Just step up and run it down. Take that hole away from the other fellow. Square the match. The opening was there and a champion—an experienced player, a real fighter—doesn't miss things like that. That other fellow probably was worrying a lot at the moment. He probably was ashamed of being short at a time like that. And he left himself a ticklish one to hole even if Lawson didn't get this birdie. But this

155

looked pretty good. It was Lawson's first chance to give his man a stiff jolt. He stood over his ball, faced his club a couple of times, and putted.

The ball rolled smoothly down the slight slope, and then the crowd gave a great collective gasp. The putt was inches wide of the cup and rolled about four feet beyond. A horrified whisper ran around the gallery. If he missed this he would be 2 down. McCullough might be the giant-killer. Maybe Lawson finally was cracking under the strain. That was a bad putt. No reason for being that much off the line—or that far past the hole. Maybe something sensational was happening under their eyes. "McCullough Defeats Little": a headline like that would be sensational. The whispering in the gallery continued.

Lawson walked slowly to the other side of the green and studied his four-footer. It would be pretty bad to miss this one. He would be 2 down. Some one of these birds would beat him some day. Maybe this was the fellow. Lawson couldn't keep on winning forever. Not at golf. It can't be done. Four-footers are mean on the best of greens. Lawson lined up his putt, faced his club, looked again, and stepped away. He stepped up again, faced his club and hit the ball. It rolled in. He looked at McCullough's ball as he stepped back from picking his own out of the hole. McCullough's ball was only sixteen inches from the cup. Well, let him hole it. This was a battle. Lawson wasn't giving anything away. Let him hole it. McCullough stepped up and holed it. The crowd streamed off to line the next fairway and the players strolled toward the sixth tee.

"What happened on that hole?" queried a late-comer to one of the stragglers from the fifth green.

"Nothing," said the straggler, rushing to catch up with the crowd. "They halved it in 3."

So nothing happened at that hole. All right, then, forget about it. But something happened once at the final hole on the great Hoylake course overseas and this is what it was:

This could have happened only in jolly old England. The famous Hoylake course is a wind-swept, seaside golf terrain near Liverpool—the "Royal Liverpool" is the high-hat name for the course—and the usual weather report for the area is "Rain, followed by storms." It's a very old club, stuffed with all honorable parts and loaded down with elderly members, stiff and starchy on the outside but "decent old chaps, oh, very!" underneath it all. Golf is practically a religion with them, and the playing of the game is a rite. The rules of the game as laid down by the Royal and Ancient are as the laws of the Medes and Persians to them. That was why they were horrified when the Oxford and Cambridge golfing societies came down there of a bad day to play their annual undergraduate matches. There was so much water in the bunkers, due to recent rains, that the carefree university captains agreed to call it "casual water," even in the bunkers, an astounding and shocking violation of the rules and traditions according to the Council of the Elders at Hoylake. They stalked into the clubhouse indignantly, steaming with wrath and uttering emphatic comments. The universities were seething hotbeds of red radicalism, by Jove! The Home Secretary should take steps. In their days the university had been a school for gentlemen and not a kennel for graceless cubs.

Thus the storm raged while the Oxford team played the Cambridge team, blandly indifferent to the con-

157

demnation of the whole proceedings by the Council of the Elders at Hoylake. But it was another day and another hand that rocked the old Hoylake club to its foundation by the pocket veto of the utterly priceless putt. Among the good amateur golfers of that era in England—about ten years ago—were the two Humphries brothers. They belonged to the younger set at Hoylake and played the game in a comparatively lighthearted way, not wayward enough to upset the elders until this fatal day on which were played the finishing rounds of a rather important medal score tournament. The elders were out in force because it was an important event, and many noted players were going over the famous course, and their medal scores would go into the archives to be preserved for posterity.

A breathless courier sped in over the wind-swept terrain with the startling news that one of the Humphries brothers was burning up the course and the old record of 70 for amateur players was in grave danger. Just which of the Humphries brothers it was, deponent sayeth not; but on this particular day he was going great guns despite wind and weather and was on the eighteenth tee with a par for a 68. Out burst the elders from the taproom of the clubhouse to witness the conclusion of such a wonderful round and the establishment of a new amateur record for the famous old course. It would be an event that would make golf history at Hoylake. It had to be properly witnessed and certified Chairs and benches were carried out and placed around the home green, and the elders took their seats as solemnly and as deeply moved as if they were witnessing a coronation in Westminster Abbey. Hardly had they seated and settled themselves with dignity when they saw the

Humphries chap play a stiff iron for his second shot over the nasty cross-bunker on the way to the green. The ball rolled up on the green and came to a stop about twelve feet from the hole.

"What does he lie?" shouted one of the grandees to those of the galloping gallery that had come up to the green with the hero.

"He has that putt for a 67!" gasped one of the runners, his voice quivering with mingled fatigue and excitement.

"A-a-ah!" said the elders in unison, and then they looked at one another in awe. Remarkable! Historical! Absolutely astounding! Every move was important now. This would be something to discuss for years to come. The smallest detail would figure in the great chronicle of golf at Hoylake.

Humphries came along with a group of reverent attendants. Even the carefree young player seemed to be sobered by the solemnity of the epoch-making occasion, the importance of that moment in golfing history. His lips were set in a grim line, and he was carrying his iron club as though it were a shining sword and he were St. George advancing to smite the dastardly dragon. He moved up on the green, and the crowd closed behind him, making the circle complete around the green. His companion's caddie went to the flagstick. Humphries glanced at his ball and called to his own caddie for a putter. The great moment was at hand!

Mind you, he was lying 66, and the hallowed amateur record that had stood for years was 70. From twelve feet away he could take three putts and still earn a great place in Hoylake history. Two putts—two very ordinary putts —would give him a 68, which would be a regular "double-oxer" by way of record-smashing on the old course. One putt for a 67. Well, it would be an act of God or at least a minor miracle and maybe too much for human hearts to ask for and human eyes to see—but the old record was doomed, a new one was in the making, and that was the great thing to see. Take it fair and easy, laddie!

Humphries knelt down behind his ball and studied the line to the hole. The silent watchers held their breaths. The whine of the wind coming in off the sea was the only audible sound, a proper orchestral accompaniment to a great golfing feat at Hoylake. Having surveyed the line from the ball to the hole, Humphries arose and walked to the far side of the green. He knelt down and sighted the line from that direction. More tension in the gallery that ringed the green. One of the elders, while this was going on, put his hand over his heart. It was pumping furiously and the dashed heart specialist had warned him against undue excitement. But—harrumph!—he couldn't miss this! The Hoylake amateur record being smashed to smithereens and he to walk away from the sight like a lily-livered coward! He would stick it, by Jove! Oh, rather!

Having surveyed the line of putt fore and aft, Humphries went to the west and east and took beam sights on the target, all very carefully. Ten minutes had passed. Perspiration was breaking out on the foreheads of the elders. The veins in their faces were beginning to stand out like whipcords. Finally Humphries went up to the ball, putter in hand, and bent over and took his stance. Everybody in the gallery leaned breathlessly forward, all eyes fixed on the little white ball. Humphries stood there with his club resting behind the ball for a

160

full minute. Then he suddenly straightened up, called to his caddie, and changed to another putter.

By George! this was nerve-racking in the extreme! Why didn't the confounded chap get on with it? Flesh and blood around the green couldn't stand up under it much longer. The elders would be toppling out of their seats and sprawling lifeless on the grass. Again Humphries took his stance, and again breathing was suspended all around. Back stepped Humphries a second time. He called his caddie and changed back to his first putter.

By this time almost everybody in the gallery was a shattered nervous wreck. Strong men felt like screaming to let off tension. The elders were staring with popping eyes and parted lips. Humphries knelt down behind his ball to take one final look at the line of putt. Then, looking around at the assembled multitude, he said in a tone of decided annoyance:

"Oh, this is far too difficult—I'll never hole it!"

And, with that, he picked up his ball, put it into his pocket, and stalked off through the horrified gallery. The Council of the Elders, of course, collapsed in a dignified body. It was the worst thing that ever happened at Hoylake.

SONG OF THE FAR-FLUNG FAIRWAYS

(Taking six strokes from Rudyard Kipling)

"The white moth to the closing bine,
The bee to the opened clover."
And the mashie pitch to the ghastly ditch,
Ever the wide world over.

"Ever the wide world over, lad,
Clear to the Arctic zone."
By the glacial ice you can see the slice
And hear the duffer moan.

There are greens by the Guadalquivir;
Fairways in old Cathay;
And a tough tenth hole that will sear your soul
On the road to Mandalay.

"The wild boar to the sun-dried swamp;
The red crane to her reed."
And an easy par at Kandahar
Is a lure for the golfing breed.

There's a nine-hole course at Quito
With greens that fringe the sky,
And they cut the grass in the Khyber Pass
To furnish a brassie lie.

By the wash of the Parramatta
Is the golfing flag unfurled,
And the feet of the dub—and the marks of his club—
Make a trail around the world.

Just after the first flurry of snow in December there arrived the following letter, the full import of which can be grasped only in households where "paterfamilias" is of the true golfing clan; but the revelations contained therein may serve as a bar or warning against a spread of the infection:

Dear Sir:

I thought you'd like to know that Father is home again. The golf links closed for the season yesterday. He isn't the same man who left here last spring. He went out of a windy morning in late March with a new bag of clubs, a joyous step, high hope in his heart, and lofty ambition in his soul.

Before he left he said: "I've got it now. It's simple. I wonder how I went wrong all these years. Now, see here. Notice how my wrists are? That's wrong. They should be like this. [Business of showing how.] As I go through the ball, I pronate properly. The wrists, ladies and gentlemen, are the—"

Mother cut in there and said that reminded her she had to make some applesauce herself, so she walked away. But Father kept right on. He mentioned something about elbows and keeping them close to the body. Hit from the inside out: that was the trick. He had been hitting from the outside in, which was why he had found golf an expensive game.

So Dorothy said: "Speaking of expenses, Dad, I must have a new hat. Will you leave the money before you go?" And he said, "No!" and she left. But Father just went on talking. "I'll add twenty yards to my drive," he said, "and what I'll do to those bandits at the club will be plenty, with compound interest. You are looking at a man who will never top another iron shot in the course of his natural life. Hit the ball down! Bang it as though you meant to knock it through to China. That's the secret of getting the ball up. You can't miss. You can't lose. Bearing that firmly in mind, a man could pile up a snug fortune at the slow but steady rate of twenty-five cents per hole. That's our union scale at the club. Why, I remember I was playing the twelfth hole one day and my drive was—"

163

So then everybody walked away. His voice kept going for about ten minutes and then stopped, as if in surprise or indignation. Next thing we heard was the door slamming. He was gone. That was in March. And he just came back. Metaphorically speaking, he came in on his hands and knees. The bottom was out of his bag, his driver was missing, the shaft of his midiron was split, all his iron clubs were covered with rust, and his spirit was about as firm as an ill-used dishrag.

It seems that his short cut to golf glory was no go. His various discoveries and inventions backfired and blew his score sky-high. When he concentrated on one thing, he forgot everything else, with the result that the ball went off at astonishing angles. He tried to hit the ball into the ground. Worse still, he succeeded. He shattered six shafts of his iron clubs before he admitted his error. Instead of adding twenty yards to his drive, he added twenty strokes to his score. He was in the woods so much he admitted he should have had a bird dog rather than a caddie with him. His driver, he threw into the middle of the pond at the fourth hole. It was the longest distance he got with that club all year.

Well, we were sure he was cured. He didn't dare to open his mouth for hours. He threw his clubs into a closet and sat down with a horribly guilty look on his face. And you know why— man of his age, deserting his family, futile pastime. Why worry about golf? Life is real, life is earnest—all that sort of thing. We left him alone with his bitter thoughts.

About a half-hour afterward we found him standing in the center of the rug on the living-room floor. He had a midiron in his hand and was making mysterious motions with it. So Mother said, "I'm surprised, Jim!" and he said: "I'm surprised myself. It just came to me this minute. By jiminy! That's the real secret. I've got it at last. I'll rig up a practice net in the attic, and when they open those links again I'll knock those other fellows dead!"

So Mother said, somewhat bitterly, I thought, "I hope you do, and vice versa." But I doubt that Father heard her. He was on the way up to the attic to fix up his practice net. And nothing can be done about it.

Sorrowfully yours, &c.

164

No, nothing can be done. Furthermore, self-instruction—or the delusion that passes as such—in golf is a mild and localized form of insanity compared to the wave of hysteria that engulfs thousands of fanatics when they come upon a new book or new method or new man suddenly revealing the secret of success at the old game—and offering the same for sale on a wide scale. When the fever is at its height, the books, lectures, or hours of instruction by the latest discoverer of the secret of success at golf go like hot cakes. Clever fellows, these super-professors of golf. They keep up with the times. A century ago they would have reaped a goodly harvest selling patent medicines off the back end of a wagon. As for the feat of producing, by instruction, a set of pupils slamming out one perfect shot after another, there is the alleged account of the work of such a wizard that might be offered by way of light warning.

Once on a battle-scarred fairway, hard by a thrice-bunkered green,
Sandy McNab of Carnoustie teaching his pupils was seen.
Perfect and peerless instructor, his method of teaching was such,
Slicing was cured with a gesture, hooking was cured with a touch.
Ultimate dream of all golfers, a magical method to learn;
Sandy made each of his pupils a master of par in his turn.
Topping and shanking he banished, perfect his pupils became.
Hear what became of poor Sandy! Hark how he ruined the game!

As a matter of fact, Sandy was warned against what he was doing; but the Scots are a stubborn folk. You see, Sandy knew all about golf. He wasn't the world's greatest player, but he was the world's greatest teacher. You've met those fellows. They bob up wherever there are golf courses and bewildered duffers who will listen to any one who talks nonsense about golf with an air of authority. They can analyze swings, draw charts, discourse at length on pronating, and orate until the cows come home on such important topics as "The Left Hand at the Top of the Slice" or "The Influence of the Right Wrist on Short Holes." One of these self-admitted wizards may have inveigled you into a dark room where, with electric lights on your feet, knees, wrists, shoulders, and head, you were requested to swing and be photographed in the process. When the plates were developed, your swinging motions —all horribly wrong—were exposed as whirling white lines on a black background. Your faults were pointed out by the professor, and you were handed a chart of instructions. If you practiced assiduously and according to the chart, within a month you were enabled to increase your average score by ten or twelve strokes. It is merely mentioned in passing that, if a man gave the same concentrated mental attention to the simple and natural act of swallowing food that he is urged to give to the simple act of swinging a golf club, the chances are that he would choke to death on the first mouthful that went down his gullet. Why a civilized government pursues a little thing like the Japanese beetle relentlessly and permits these greater golf pests to flourish and prosper, is a matter that intelligent taxpayers should take up with their Congressmen.

But Sandy McNab, to be sure, was different. He was what the others claimed to be, the perfect instructor. Some say that Perfection is a dream. Some say it's a mild cigar. Some insist that it was a good brand of whiskey when they last tasted it. But Sandy McNab arrived at

Perfection in golf, and among those who detest the royal and ancient game his name ever will be venerated.

As Sandy said, there are many ways of hitting a golf ball, but there is only one perfect way. He experimented until he found that perfect way. Then he tried various methods of instruction until he found the one perfect way of teaching the perfect golf stroke. The result was as logical as the construction of the Wonderful One-Hoss Shay. The ultimate crash was just as logical and complete.

All this happened on a large and well populated island where golf was the favorite game of the inhabitants and good courses and fine tournaments abounded. The name and location of the island are kept secret because of the frightful catastrophe that followed, and because somebody might try to rescue Sandy from the dark dungeon in which he has been chained ever since for his perfect crime. The only geographical hint that will be given is the simple statement that the island is entirely surrounded by water.

You see, Sandy was too perfect. He put forward his claims as a golf instructor, capable of teaching the perfect stroke, and the careless inhabitants thought he was just another of those "witch doctors" of the game who know everything about golf except how to play it themselves. But Sandy showed them he could teach it perfectly. That was the worst of it. No sooner did he take charge of a class of ten pupils than the reaching fingers of Fate were around the golf shafts of that island. The full hand of Fate came down with crushing force later.

It had to be. There were twelve in this class and all were graduated "summa cum laude." They had been taught the perfect stroke by the perfect master, and the result was ambulating perfection on the course. They couldn't miss a shot. Nobody could beat them. However, one peculiar but logical thing became apparent immediately. They couldn't beat one another. (Dramatic forecast!) When one graduate of the McNab School of Perfect Golf met another alumnus, the strokes were perfect and parallel, and the match was square all the way. There was no point in carrying on for extra holes, because the same logical situation prevailed.

So the McNab alumni sought other golfing rivals and beat them with monotonous regularity. Naturally, that led to a run on the McNab School of Perfect Golf. Desirous of spreading golf education and not averse to swelling the McNab bank account, Sandy took them in as fast as they came. In time, they were graduated as perfect golfers. With his system, no one could miss. In short, like maddened migrating lemmings leaping into the sea, all the golfers on the island finally passed through the McNab School of Perfect Golf. The approaching catastrophe is now apparent to any logical mind. What would become of doctors in any country where, by the curative skill of the medical men themselves, all the inhabitants had been put into a state of perfect health? Alas for Sandy McNab, who taught golf not wisely but too well.

The answer is self-evident. For a brief and bewildering time the golfers of the island tried to continue, but it wouldn't do. Every player was perfect. No one could win a match or even a hole. Of course, McNab had no more pupils and his income fell off to nothing; but that was a minor matter over which the angered inhabitants wasted no thought at all. The last attempt to carry on was in the holding of the island championship. In the qualifying

168

round at thirty-six holes every golfer on the island turned in a score of 144, perfect par. The committee decided to go ahead at match play, with everybody still in. No use. All matches were all square all the way.

"Gentlemen," said the Governor-General of the island, himself one of the contestants, "we have reached an impasse. We should have remembered the words of Wolsey when he said: 'Cromwell, I charge thee, fling away ambition!' We have been ruined by ambition. We all wanted to be perfect golfers, and we are! Now our lives are blighted. Our game is ruined. There is nothing to do but fling away our clubs and plow up our courses. We will invent a new game, and, whatever form that new game may take, in a thoroughly humble spirit I suggest that no one be allowed to take or give lessons in that game. We can all say, in all sadness, that we have had our lesson."

"And what of McNab?" screamed an indignant citizen.

"Throw the scoundrel into the dungeon under the watch tower," ordered the Governor-General, "and let him never escape to blight golf in any other territory."

Since golf is happily imperfect through the rest of the world, it is presumed that the talented but luckless McNab still languishes in durance vile on the island where he perfected and ruined the game.

Perfection, bah! Walter Hagen wasn't perfect on the links. Sam Snead isn't perfect. Nor Gene Sarazen. Not even the Emperor Jones. Not even the late Harry Vardon, the Old Master of vanished years. Apropos of Vardon, who smoked a pipe and wasted few words on the links, he was playing with Bob Jones in the United

169

States open championship at Inverness, just outside Toledo, Ohio, in 1920. Young Bob—he was only eighteen at the time—had been chattering cheerfully as he went along. Vardon just kept on puffing his pipe. At the seventh hole Jones had a very easy shot to the green for his second. He could almost have kicked the ball up there. But he used a club and mistreated the ball horribly. It dribbled ahead a few dozen yards. Blushing, Bob turned and said to his companion:

"Mister Vardon, did you ever see a worse shot?"

Taking his pipe out of his mouth as if to give the matter some thought, Vardon said:

"No."

Then he put his pipe into his mouth and went on with his own game.

So the great ones of the fairway have had and do have their faults, and golf is the better game for it. In 1929 the Emperor Jones was playing in the open championship over the Winged Foot course at Mamaroneck, New York, and had the tournament in hand with nine holes to go. He thereupon proceeded to put on a display of golf that reduced his royal rooters to a body of shuddering wrecks. Any one would have bet that Jones couldn't be that bad with one hand tied behind his back. But he was, and countless thousands mourned. However, there was a happy ending. After all his waywardness, after all the strokes he had frittered away, he stumbled up to the last green with a sidehill putt of perhaps twelve feet to tie Al Espinosa's leading score of 294.

Mike Brady, the home-club pro, was standing on a chair, looking over the heads of the human ring that encircled the green.

"How does it look, Mike?" queried a friend on the ground who couldn't see what was going on. Mike shook his head and said:

"Bad. He'll never hole that one."

A great shout went up from the crowd.

"By God!" yelled Mike. "He held it!"

Which he did, and went on the next day to beat Espinosa by twenty-three strokes in the thirty-six-hole play-off for the championship. So even a golfer like the Emperor Jones varied from day to day. Old George Low, the esteemed and even beloved professional at Baltusrol for so many years, once said—by the way, the club pros who give good solid instructions to members of their own clubs are not to be confused with the wandering "witch doctors" who profess to be able to cure every golfer in the world of all his faults—well, George Low, out of the depths of his experience, once said:

"Golf is a humblin' game!"

So it is. But it's a hopeful game, too. Otherwise the suffering duffers would turn to something else in a hurry. But they return to the links relentlessly, filled with a spirit that once brought the following words from the depths of a tortured heart:

TOMORROW!

(Starting 18 down to John Masefield)

Oh, yesterday, flushed high with hope, I stood upon the tee.
My drive I hooked behind a rock; my second hit a tree;
And all the dreadful afternoon I flubbed in misery.
But tomorrow, by the gods of golf! I'll try the game again!

Oh, yesterday my heart was torn with top and slice and hook;
The wayward path I followed led by rough and trap and brook;
And as I missed the tenth short putt, my soul in anguish shook.
But tomorrow, by the Great Horn Spoon! I'll try the game again!

Oh, yesterday I drenched the course with bitter scalding tears,
And what I said of golf I hope will never reach your ears.
I swore I wouldn't touch a club for years and years and years.
But tomorrow—you can bet on this!—I'll try the game again!

ON THE FOOTBALL FIELD

THE OLD TACKLE SLANT

*"Why don't you give our team a break?" the Dartmouth rooter
   cried,*
"You're pushing Fordham to the fore and shoving us aside;
You write of Pittsburgh, Harvard, Yale, Columbia and more,
And Princeton space is double, which I very much deplore.
Apparently you've never learned that Dartmouth's on the map.
So take this hint, which, entre nous, is just a verbum sap."

*"Why don't you give our team a break?" the Fordham rooter
   said,*
"You fill a page with Harvard stuff that leaves me seeing red.
You rant of Navy, Notre Dame, of Dartmouth every day;
But not a word of Fordham as it goes its winning way.
This slight upon the Old Maroon must be a deep-laid plot.
Unless you change, I'll cancel my subscription on the spot!"

"Why don't you give our team a break?" the Navy rooter writes,
"You boom the Army to the skies in fancy verbal flights,
With columns full of Army mules and Kaydet monkeyshines,
And then submerge the Navy with three dinky agate lines.
It's really quite preposterous the prejudice you show.
The Navy has your number, and I thought you ought to know."

And so it goes on every side, the great autumnal gale
Of loud complaint from Oregon, Ohio State and Yale,
From Stanford and Columbia, from Michigan and Maine,

From East and West and North and South, the cry of woe and
  pain.
The volume is tremendous, but the helpful records show
That it falls away to silence with the first December snow.

IT CERTAINLY is odd how the loyal alumnus always feels that his alma mater is being neglected in the public prints when the football season is on. There is no other game that sweeps its followers along at such hysterical heights—or lets them down more quickly after the last point has been kicked for the year. It may be that, in the future, the rising popularity of professional football will lessen the fiery fury of the undergraduate or alumnus for his college team. After all, the professionals in the big league do put on a more powerful game of football. The college background, the college colors, the co-ed touch, the aura of traditional rivalry and campus affiliations of that kind are missing from the professional field. But if it's just football that the crowd wants—the jury is still out—the great games of the future will be played by paid postgraduate performers wearing the uniforms of the Chicago Bears, the Washington Redskins, the Green Bay Packers, the New York Giants, or some other organization dedicated to the production of profitable public spectacles rather than to the pursuit of higher education.

But the college game—come what may in the future —is still the main attraction. To the Rose Bowl game as the climax of the season there have been added the Sugar Bowl, the Cotton Bowl, and the Orange Bowl games, in which the leading teams of the college year go all out for post-season glory—and the share of the gate receipts that is no small inducement. Further than that, and no matter how the tide of college football supremacy may

174

swing in seasonal variations, traditional games still draw great crowds. Army and Navy may be "nowhere" in national ranking, and Yale and Harvard may be beaten by three or four—or more—rivals, but the Army-Navy game will find purchasers eagerly bidding for tickets that are not to be had for love or money and great crowds always will flock to the Harvard Stadium or the Yale Bowl when the Bulldog meets the Crimson on the grid-iron. Tradition is strong on the field of sports, and college football, beyond any other sport, is bolstered and upholstered by ivy-covered tradition.

Having watched hundreds of big football games in a quarter of a century of eager observation, I here confess that the greatest thrill came from the playing of a game almost three thousand miles away. In the season of 1933 Stanford had a great team on the Coast and was named to defend the honor of the Pacific Coast in the Rose Bowl game at Pasadena on January 1, 1934. What eastern team would get the bid was the big question. Army had a great team that year. So did Duke. Columbia started with a fine squad and great prospects, but overconfidence gave Lou Little's Lions a terrific setback. In an early season game against Princeton, which had a corking team that year, too, Columbia fumbled the opening kick-off, was thrown backward in haste by the joyous Tigers and took a lopsided beating, 20–0. So Columbia was crossed off the list.

Princeton swept on to one triumph after another and could have had the Rose Bowl bid on a silver platter, but the old "Big Three" of Yale, Harvard and Princeton had an agreement against taking part in such post-season festivities. Duke went along undefeated to the last game,

175

which was against Georgia Tech. Army marched over all rivals up to the final game against Notre Dame in the Yankee Stadium in New York, beating Yale, Harvard, Illinois, and other good teams en route. Only thirteen points had been scored against Army in all those games. Stanford and the football fans of the Coast would have been delighted to entertain the Army football team—the whole corps of Cadets, for that matter—in the Rose Bowl. But on that last bitter day in the Yankee Stadium the Notre Dame team beat the Army 13–12 and, off in a southerly direction, Georgia Tech shoved the Duke team down to defeat by 6–0. Now Columbia had won all its games except that clash with Princeton and, at the close of the season, seemed about as powerful and well drilled an outfit as any eastern football follower could hope to see in action. With the downfall of Army and Duke and the knowledge that Princeton wouldn't entertain a bid, there came the bewildering switch. The Columbia team had disbanded. Coach Little had gone off somewhere to bury his head in his hands and think of what a season it might have been except for the fumble of that opening kick-off at Princeton. Then the telephone rang at Columbia University. Rose Bowl calling.

Columbia didn't leap at the invitation. The faculty council on athletics debated the matter. The football followers debated the matter, too. Of course, the fans decided immediately and unanimously that Columbia should accept the bid—and almost immediately and unanimously that the great Stanford team would tan the hides of the Lions in the Rose Bowl encounter. While the faculty members were still weighing the invitation, the situation was set forth as follows:

176

The eastern Coach, with all his staff,
Was standing in the hall.
The Rose Bowl bid was in, and they
Were waiting for the call.
The faculty was huddling and
The Dean still held the ball.

"If twenty men we used against
Eleven on their side,
Do you suppose," the Head Coach said,
"That Stanford could be tied?"
"I doubt it!" groaned an aide-de-camp,
And broke right down and cried.

"If all our men wore armor plate
With rivets at the seam,
We still might save the lives of all
The players on our team,"
The Head Coach said. But that seemed just
A hopeful eastern dream.

There rose a wailing, warning voice
The coaching staff amid:
"From fire and from pestilence
Please keep the East safe hid,
From famine and from slaughter and
From Bowl of Roses bid!"

That was all in fun, of course, and Coach Lou Little wasn't really standing in the hall surrounded by a quivering staff as the faculty debated the acceptance or refusal of the Stanford invitation, which, to unprejudiced ears, sounded strangely like the old nursery jingle of "Daffy, Daffy, come and be killed." As a matter of fact, Coach Little was seated calmly at his desk in John Jay Hall, answering or parrying questions that seemed pertinent or impertinent at the time. He was calm enough, but the calmness seemed to be of the-condemned-man-ate-a-hearty-breakfast type.

"Do you know," said a heckler, "what happens to good little eastern teams that go to the Rose Bowl?"

"Oh, I know they have great football teams out there," countered Mr. Little.

"The better to eat you up with, my dear," said the heckler mockingly. "Bowl of Roses invitation! Beware of the Greeks bringing gifts."

"So far as I know," said Coach Little, "there isn't a Greek on the Stanford squad."

"Columbia is the gem of the Atlantic Ocean," continued the heckler, "but the Pacific is a bigger body of water. Those Princeton boys were smart, turning up

their noses at Stanford. I'll bet those Princeton boys were all Phi Beta Kappa men. They knew better than to be dragged around a Bowl of Roses and come out all scratched up. Aren't you interested in the physical welfare of your boys? Why, those Stanford giants will come in grunting, 'Fee, fie, fo, fum! I smell the blood—' "

"Just a minute!" protested Coach Little, half rising from his chair. "I'm still hale and hearty, and I went out there with Penn in 1917 and played in one of those games."

"Who won?"

"Oh, well," said Coach Little, "we lost—but we saved our lives."

Just then a messenger rushed in with word that Coach Little was wanted at the faculty conference. He went. The invitation had been accepted. Columbia was going to battle the great Stanford team in the Rose Bowl. What a Columbia halfback might be thinking during the successive shocks of that fearful fray there was no way of knowing as yet; but a guess at it was made and dropped on Lou Little's desk in the following form:

Tell me not of mournful numbers meaning I must take the ball
And be picked up crushed and breathless underneath that Stanford wall.
Life is tough (and this is earnest), and it's hard to reach your goal
With a guard like Corbus waiting where there isn't any hole.

Eastern teams that went before us left this lesson that we learn;
That there is no time for spinners when there isn't room to turn;
That an eastern tackle cutback simply isn't in the cards
When the best men in your backfield are two stalwart Stanford guards!

And those speedy Stanford runners! They come shooting through the line
And, departing, leave behind them footprints up and down your spine.
Let us then be up and going; run the next play to the gate;
Let them gather all the roses while we catch an eastbound freight.

What! You still insist on playing? Woe is me! I'll take the ball,
And if you survive the massacre, my dying words recall.
Moriturus te saluto! For Columbia I roar!
And tell them to remember me but please forget the score.

This was set down in good clean fun and friendly fear that the Lions would be much overmatched in the Pasadena festivities. The Pitt Panthers had gone out there three times before that and, after each trip, it was a month's job pulling all the thorns out of the Panther fur. Except for fair Harvard in 1920, that won on the Coast by the narrowest of legal margins, a thin point, the best that any eastern team had achieved out there was a breathless tie.

Columbia had a great eleven—and not much more. Stanford had a great eleven, and plenty of powerful reserves. It was conceded that the Columbia first team, good men, beautifully drilled, would give a fine account of itself—as long as it could carry on. But when the overpowering Stanford reserves were poured in against the weary Columbia regulars, what was going to happen?

"That's what we're going to find out," said Coach Little as he went off to collect his warriors who had scattered after the close of the eastern football season. There was snow all over the East. The Columbia squad had to work indoors until the time came, during the Christmas holidays, to entrain for the Coast. The weather was beautiful in California. The Stanford squad continued to work out on turf, bathed in crisp sunlight.

However, the Stanford players didn't think they would need to practice very much to beat Columbia. It looked like a push-over. Coach Tiny Thornhill tried to tell them that Columbia was coming out with a dangerous team, but they didn't take him seriously. The hardest part of their preparation for the great day was posing for pictures and autographing the same for distribution among their California admirers, whose name was legion. The hardest job of the Pasadena promoters of the Rose Bowl football party was to persuade the local citizenry that the slaughter of the little squad from Columbia by the great Stanford horde would be worth the price of admission.

That was the real tip-off on the public rating of Columbia's chances in the Rose Bowl; it was hard to sell tickets for the game. Even with good weather and California's enthusiasm for football, nobody expected the Rose Bowl to be filled.

Well, it was filled in one way. It was filled with water the day before the game. The rains came. The countryside was flooded. The first look that Coach Lou Little had at the Rose Bowl gridiron disclosed it as a submerged playground. Fire-engine pumps were put to work and the water was removed, but the gridiron was in such shape that Tiny Thornhill, the Stanford coach, wanted to postpone the game. Lou Little was for playing it, come hell or high water. Maybe, as some sarcastic Californians hinted, he dreaded it and wanted to get it over with. In any case, Coach Little stuck to his guns and it was decided to play, as scheduled, on New Year's Day. So, with clouds swirling across the sky and some rain still falling, the mighty Stanford squad and the little band of invaders from New York trotted out on a very sloppy field on this inauspicious New Year's Day and, with the Rose Bowl hardly half filled with spectators, began the game that will long be remembered in football history.

Right from the start the radio listeners back in the East knew that fun was afoot. The altogether too self-satisfied Stanford stalwarts were unceremoniously jolted by the underrated Easterners. Those Stanford adherents and California neighbors who had turned out to watch a triumphal parade put on by their heroes sat back open-mouthed, eyes wide in absolute horror. Could such things be? Every time Columbia made a gain, which was frequently, the radio announcers spoke of it tentatively as though it were something they probably would have to take back later on. And, to tell the truth, that was also the feeling of the listeners back home in the East. What was going on seemed to be too good to last.

But it did last through the first period. There was no score, but Columbia was forcing the fighting. Stanford had been staggered by this unexpected charge of the invaders from the East and was having a hard time settling down to real work. For instance, in the second period the Columbia forwards surged through and blocked a Stanford punt. Stanford luckily recovered but had to kick again from farther back. That was the way the game was going. Then Cliff Montgomery, the great little Columbia quarterback, tossed off a forward pass to Red Matal at end, and Matal carried it to Stanford's 17-yard line. Half a minute later there was a Columbia spinner play—the now famous "KF-79"—that left the Stanford players wondering what ever became of the ball. They grabbed at one man and another, and each time it was all a mistake. It was all too late when they looked off to the right and saw Left Halfback Barabas of Columbia galloping alone and unhampered across the goal line. The point was kicked and it was 7–0 in favor of Columbia.

What Coach Thornhill said to his discomfited Stanford squad between the halves must have been plenty, for they came out determined to make Columbia pay for that insolence. But Columbia was high, too. They had their touchdown. Let those other fellows try to match it. And Stanford tried and failed. Bob Grayson and Bones Hamilton, their great backs, plunged fiercely or slanted swiftly for good gains. Six times they were in scoring position, but six times Columbia held. Once Stanford had a first down on Columbia's 3-yard line. At the fourth

down it was Columbia's ball on the 1-yard line. Countless thousands of eastern football followers were hunched
over in chairs drawn close up to blaring radios. Stanford
was really banging away. After hurling back all those
assaults, could the short-handed Columbia squad hold
that precious lead to the finish? If they could, what an
upset! What a tremendous victory! Last few minutes
to play. Stanford again pounding down toward the
Columbia goal. At the 20-yard line. At the 10-yard line.
Columbia held again. Escape! Then a little more skir-
mishing, and a shot was heard. The game was over.
Columbia—the team that didn't have a chance—had scored
a great victory, merited all the way. The Rose Bowl spectators went home in a daze. To them it was as if they
had seen a lamb slay a butcher.

Naturally there was a big celebration for the conquering Columbia heroes when they returned to New York
and, with the feeling that some special apology was due
from a prophet of gloom, there was offered for the occasion the following heartfelt

BALLADE OF JOYOUS ERROR

Oh, Lions triumphant, here be it proclaimed,
I fell for the fables the Coast folk relate;
I trembled lest friends should be horribly maimed,
And "Mercy upon us!" was all I could prate.
Barabas and Monty—Brominski, his mate—
Bill Corbus would crush them in tentacles strong;
Bob Grayson would circle them, light-foot, elate;
I laughed with delight when you proved I was wrong.

Ah, little you'd save where the big battle flamed
(Lou Little, perhaps, if he hid near the gate);
By thorns in the Rose Bowl you boys would be lamed

185

And halted and crippled—a sight I would hate.
So this filtered out through the crack in my pate—
I muttered, in short, what they shouted so long:
"Ride out in a Pullman and home in a crate!"
I laughed with delight when you proved I was wrong.

The Panthers bloodthirsty like tabbies were tamed,
And Stanford was harder to stop than a freight
(All these were the stories that had me outgamed);
The East was a set-up, beyond all debate.
His paws in a pickle, his head on a plate,
The Lion they'd serve to a Native Son throng;
For you, just a tombstone—"Hic Jacet!" and date;
I laughed with delight when you proved I was wrong.

L'Envoi

Lou—meaning Coach Little—this lightens my fate,
And this is the lilt that enlivens my song:
It's bright to be right, but this time I must state,
I laughed with delight when you proved I was wrong.

It was a few days later that Coach Lou Little, going from one Columbia celebration to another, said:

"I'm having more fun after this trip to the Coast than I did after the first trip out there." So that story came out, too.

It was in 1917 that Penn, the outstanding team of the East, received a Rose Bowl bid and accepted. Oregon was the defending team for the Coast and, in the game, made a good job of it by beating Penn 14–0. Lou Little was one of the best players in the Pennsylvania line. He said he enjoyed everything about the game except the score. Aside from that, his California visit was a pleasure.

186

It was on the way back that he sank into gloom. Examinations were coming up as soon as the football players returned to college and, through concentrating on football during the Rose Bowl expedition, Student Little feared he had lost his grip on certain classical subjects. He longed for a postponement, if possible, to give him time to prepare for the stiff examinations.

He mentioned this to some of his football cronies on the train that was carrying them back to Philadelphia, and they came through with various suggestions in which Student Little saw more mirth than solid matter. But one fellow really had a bright idea.

"Go sick," he said. "Think up some excuse for getting into the infirmary, and they'll give you a postponement of your examinations."

"What!" said Lou with a snort of disgust. "A football player claiming he's sick! Do I look sick? What a chance! Think up another."

"Well, have some minor operation," suggested his friend. "Ever have your tonsils out? No? Well, you're set. That'll do the trick. It's a cinch."

"Crickey!" said Student Little. "I believe you're right. That'll give me a week, at least. I'll try it."

When he reached college he went over to the medical building where the head man was a distinguished surgeon of foreign extraction. This eminent medico, by request, peered down the football player's throat and agreed that the tonsils were ripe for the plucking. The job could be done immediately.

But as Lou was being wheeled into the operating room he began to have some doubts about this method of getting a postponement of examinations. For one thing, he remembered that, during a previous operation for the removal of his appendix, it had been discovered that he was "a bad ether patient." He thought he ought to warn the tonsil-removal anesthetist about this. He looked up. A woman anesthetist was at his side. The distinguished surgeon of foreign extraction was over by another table, picking out his knives, grappling hooks, and other implements of torture.

"Lady," said Lou, "watch out when you switch from the gas to the ether. I'm liable to wake right up. Ether doesn't take with me."

"Yes, yes," said the woman anesthetist soothingly. "We'll take good care of you."

She called a couple of orderlies who put some straps on the large Mr. Little, binding him firmly to his rolling table. The lady fed him the gas, and he fell asleep. A bit later the lady switched to the ether. Just what Lou had feared came to pass. He was wide awake again.

"Is it all over?" he asked the lady anesthetist.

"There, there!" she said, pushing the ether cone down over his face, "Breathe deeply, breathe—"

"Hey, wait!" yelled Lou, yanking his head aside. "Cut this out! This'll be murder!"

"Breathe deeply," said the woman anesthetist again, trying to get the ether cone back where it belonged.

"Wait!" shouted Lou, struggling to get loose. "I've changed my mind. I don't want my tonsils out!"

The football patient twisted, struggled, turned, yanked, and finally got one leg loose. The table began to roll across the floor, propelled by this free Little leg. The woman anesthetist, on the run, tried to keep up with it and keep the ether cone over the ingrate's face. An orderly came up to help. Lou reached out and kicked him in the midriff, sending the interloper reeling into a glass case filled with expensive surgical apparatus. The case toppled over with a crash. Another orderly threw himself on the battling football player.

"Hold him!" roared the distinguished medical man of foreign extraction, "He'll wreck the building!"

More orderlies rushed up and, after a terrific struggle that left the operating room looking as if it had been the scene of a violent explosion, Student Little finally was put to sleep and his tonsils extracted. When it was all over and Lou was about to be discharged from the infirmary, the distinguished head man of foreign extraction came into his room, shook a warning finger at him, and said:

"Don't you ever come into this building again!"

"If I do," said Lou, "you can cut my head off."

But the operation was a success. The examinations had been postponed, and Lou had time to study up and pass them. Still, that was taking them the hard way.

One thing about football is that the game and its followers are weatherproof. Great crowds will sit in rain, snow, sleet, and high winds in the Yale Bowl or some such place and watch the struggle below on ground that may be frozen hard or ankle-deep in slime. Dartmouth played one famous game at Princeton in the snow. Ducky Pond got his nickname in a waterlogged game between Harvard and Yale in the Harvard Stadium. It was one of those mud-plastered pastimes that inspired the following lines offered with deep apologies to the estate of Sir A. Conan Doyle, who wrote the really stirring original verse—it described an incident on the Somme in the first World War—in the same meter and under the same title, to wit:

WHEN THE GUARDS CAME THROUGH

The close of a rainy day;
The edge of a rainy night;
And we at the end of a bruising fray
With a victory in sight.
We huddled and got the call;
The quarterback gave it quick;
And I was to hold the ball,
And Jim was to make the kick.
Down I crouched in my place,
And the pass was fair and true;
But I was flat on my frozen face
And I was just a hospital case
When the guards came through!

Wet to our weary knees,
Mud to our blinking eyes,
Shivering lest we freeze,
Still we could hear the cries:
"Win for the Gold and Blue!"
That's what we tried to do!
But the wickedest crime of modern time
Was the way I was smothered in choking slime
When the guards came through!

Ho! One came in with a crash,
A blundering human tank!
Hi! One came in with a dash,
A touch of swagger and swank,
An air of How-d'ya-do!
And Fancy-meeting-you!
And what became of the bally ball I never really knew,
For the world was ended and I was dead;
They broke my heart and they broke my head
When the guards came through!

INDOORS AND OUT

THE man who wants to keep in close touch with the big events in half a dozen sports in a comfortable way during the winter season couldn't do better than move into Madison Square Garden in New York and stay there by the week. The big indoor fights are held there. The National Hockey League has two teams, the Rangers and Americans, using the Garden rink as home ice. The biggest track meets of the winter are run off there. College basketball draws bigger crowds there than anywhere else in the country. Basketball teams from all over the country—from California, Texas, the Carolinas, and New England—take part in the double-headers that find picked teams from far off competing against the best that the New York colleges have to offer before roaring crowds that strain the capacity of the huge arena.

The way they handle things at the Garden is one of the marvels of modern efficiency. On a Friday night there may be a fight for the lightweight or welterweight championship of the world. The ring is solidly installed. Ringside seats cover the floor. The place is packed. Go back there the next night—Saturday night—and it looks like an entirely different place. The ring and ringside seats have vanished. A big indoor track meet—the Knights of Columbus Games or the New York A.C. Games, or the A.A.U. or Intercollegiate indoor championships—is

afoot. The infield has a board straightaway laid down for the sprint races and hurdles. There's one place for the high jumpers and another for the pole vaulters. An eleven-lap (to the mile) banked board track is there for the fastest milers in the world—or close to it. And another capacity crowd is there to follow another sport.

Go back again on Sunday night, and the level floor below the permanent seats is a wonderful surface of ice, a big-league hockey rink. And another and entirely different crowd is there to cheer for a different sport. Go back there again on Monday night—four nights in a row —and it will be basketball that has changed the scene and brought a still different clientele to fill all the seats in the place. Where the ring was, where the track athletes went over the hurdles, where the Canadian-born hockey stars whirled over a smooth stretch of ice, there is now a wooden floor laid down for the college basketball teams of the evening. The baskets have glass backboards

so the fans in the seats at the ends of the arena will have no part of their view of the game blocked off.

When Madison Square Garden was built it was on the supposition that prize fights and six-day bicycle races

195

would make it profitable. The six-day race went completely out of favor. In boxing, the promoters have to give so much to the main bout performers that there's little left for the house. In fact, the boxing privilege was finally "farmed out" to Promoter Mike Jacobs to relieve the Garden officials of always wasting time and often wasting money on it. It is ice hockey, totally unsuspected by the late Tex Rickard when he was drawing plans for the building, that has been the biggest money-maker for Madison Square Garden. Basketball is an added happy feature from the financial standpoint, and the track meets help, too. But hockey was the profitable surprise.

When hockey promoters from Canada tried to interest Rickard in having rink equipment included in his new Madison Square Garden so that hockey could be played there, he didn't know what hockey was. He asked a friend. "Oh, hockey?" said his friend. "You can't have that in the Garden. It's played on horseback." However, it was explained by the Canadian visitors that it was played on skates and might be a popular attraction in New York. To make sure that he wouldn't be out of pocket in any wild scheme, Rickard made the backers of the New York Americans, the first home team in the new Garden, put up the money to install the ice machinery. The rest of the story is known. The swift game on ice has been a sparkling success in the arena from which it was almost barred by ignorance of its eye-filling and breath-taking appeal. As for its appeal, a personal opinion is registered as follows:

> There's this that I like about hockey, my lad;
>   It's a clattering, battering sport.
> As a popular pastime it isn't half bad
>   For chaps of the sturdier sort.

STOWE

You step on the gas and you let in the clutch;
You start on a skate and come back on a crutch;
Your chance of surviving is really not much;
   It's something like storming a fort.

There's this that I like about hockey, my boy;
   There's nothing about it that's tame.
The whistle is blown and the players deploy;
   They start in to maul and to maim.
There's a dash at the goal and a crash on the ice;
The left wing goes down when you've swatted him twice;
And your teeth by a stick are removed in a trice;
   It's really a rollicking game.

There's this that I like about hockey, old chap;
   I think you'll agree that I'm right;
Although you may get an occasional rap,
   There's always good fun in the fight.
So toss in the puck, for the players are set;
Sing ho! for the dash on the enemy net;
And ho! for the smash as the challenge is met;
   And hey! for a glorious night!

As for the outdoor scene in northern winters, the landscape is all cluttered up with skiers. The Dartmouth boys had much to do with this. They encouraged the foreigners who first came over here on skis. They nourished the sport up on the Hanover hills and long ago instituted the Dartmouth Winter Carnival that grows and flourishes with increasing years—and increasing rivalry. Because the rage has spread. Probably Otto Eugen Schniebs —called Otto the Great on the ski slopes—had something to do with the spread of the "schport," as Otto calls it. In fact, Otto goes further. He said on a famous occasion: "Skiing iss more dan a schport; it iss a vay uf life!" Leader of a ski battalion in the last world war, Otto came

198

to this country as soon as he conveniently could after hostilities ceased and became the ski coach at Dartmouth. It was a great place for Schniebs, and he was just the man to fire the Dartmouth enthusiasm to greater heights and spread the gospel on skis over wider territory.

Now the "snow trains" pull out from dozens of cities across the country and ski trails stretch from Maine to Oregon and Washington. The talk on the trains is of wax and of wood, of bindings and temperature and slalom and how the snow was at Franconia Notch or Snow Valley or Lake Tahoe, and other matters that the ski-wise keep close to their hearts. There are one-day trips and week-end expeditions, and the summer hotels that once were left desolate through the winters are now kept open with fires burning and festivity all around for the entertainment—at a modest profit—of the armies of skiers now

SIXTY-YARD DASH

to be found riding the snow-covered slopes of the whole northern section of the United States.

It's grand sport; but the beginner, unless of tender age, is urged to go at it cautiously unless he is the carefree type that isn't bothered by little annoyances like a couple of broken legs.

Getting back to firmer footing and warmer weather, one person famous in track and field annals was the lone representative of 400,000,000 Chinese in the Olympic Games of 1932 at Los Angeles, California. Visiting hordes came from other countries; runners by brigades, boxers by battalions, swimmers in great shoals, sprinters by platoons, weight-throwers by the ton. The vast nation of China sent one man. This was the way of it:

> *In the month of white blossoms*
> *Did Chung Cheng-liu*
> *Leave the flowery garden*
> *By the little gate*

200

Where at twilight the Dragon sleeps,
By moonlight the nightingale sings,
And at dawn the silkworm
Feeds on the mulberry leaves.
He went by the yellow river
Where the gray cormorant
With the silver collar
Catches the foolish fish;
Out to the great sea
Went Chung Cheng-liu,
To a strange land far away,
To California called the Golden,
To the Games called Olympic,
For the glory of China.
Now we must wait.
There is bird's-nest soup
For supper.

Back in China the children were gathered in the garden, and Chang Fu, the Schoolmaster of the Bamboo Grove, read to them the verse about the Pear Tree from the book of Odes, very old. Su Tung, the Philosopher, sat under the red cedar by the little brook, thinking.

"Tell us the story of Chung Cheng-liu, the great athlete," said the children. So the Schoolmaster began:

"Willingly do I tell you the story of Chung Cheng-liu and the Games called Olympic in the far-off land of California where the sun also shines and rain falls only in golden showers at sunset when the roses are thirsty and in silver showers at night when the orange blossoms ask softly for water. Now, Chung Cheng-liu was a great runner in China and his fame spread from the snows of the North to the yellow sands of the South and even beyond. He was faster than the little fish that dart in the lake under the willows, faster than the deer on the mountain and the swallow above the plains."

202

"Li Tai Po, the great poet, always walked very slowly," said Su Tung the Philosopher, as if to himself. "I will have a cup of honorable tea. There is no hurry."

The Schoolmaster bowed deeply at the mention of Li Tai Po and continued:

"There came on the breath of the wind the tale that the great runners of the world were to strive in the land of California, and Chung Cheng-liu said, 'I will go and win for the honor of China,' and he set forth. At his parting we gathered and wished him well, and there was music from a guitar, inlaid, an ebony flute, and thirteen drums. The drums were very good. When he had departed, we went to the tomb of his honorable ancestors and strewed thereon rose petals that Chung Cheng-liu might prosper."

"Our honorable ancestors are very wise," observer Su Tung the Philosopher. "They do not run; they sleep."

The Schoolmaster bowed again and went on:

"Chung Cheng-liu traveled for days and weeks by land and sea and at last arrived in the far-off country called California, and there he found that the nations of the

world had sent many strong youths to strive for the prizes —more than the leaves on the great mulberry tree, more than the blades of grass on this lawn. And Chung Cheng-liu was all alone. I will have a cup of honorable tea myself."

The Schoolmaster sipped the honorable tea while the children waited silently. Then he went on:

"Chung Cheng-liu prepared for the first race, which was called 100 meters or about the distance from where we are sitting to the tall pine yonder that listens to the ripple of the little brook. He ate of the white of chicken and rice cakes twice-baked and the thin stalks of celery to give him strength and speed for the contest. He ran in the great arena with countless thousands of strange persons looking on. But others ran faster than he did; and the judges said to Chung Cheng-liu, 'You did not win,' and he was pained."

"Pain is the beginning of knowledge," said Su Tung the Philosopher.

"It is so," said the Schoolmaster, bowing again. "But Chung Cheng-liu would again strive for the honor of

China; and he put on his slippers with the little nails in the soles, and it was a race they called 200 meters, which is from here to the turret of the little summer-house that looks over the top of the plum tree."

"Did he win that race?" queried the smallest child softly.

"There were tall men from many nations," said the Schoolmaster. "There were men from the mountains and the seashore and the land between, and a great crowd again was gathered; and Chung Cheng-liu ran, and again they said to him, 'You did not win,' and he began to reflect."

"Reflection is the beginning of wisdom," said Su Tung the Philosopher, who was then on his third cup of honorable tea.

"There was another race," continued the Schoolmaster, "and Chung Cheng-liu put on his slippers with the little nails in the soles; and then he said to himself, 'I cannot win the Olympic Games all by myself against the runners of all the world,' and he took his shoes with the little nails in the soles and stood aside, which was wise. Nations were arrayed against him, and he was one man, alone. So he came back from far-away California and was greeted in this very garden with music from a guitar, inlaid, an ebony flute, and thirteen drums. The drums were very good. Chung Cheng-liu had done his best for China and his honorable ancestors. He was content."

"Contentment is the end of philosophy," said Su Tung the Philosopher. "If you will go away, I will sleep."

So the Schoolmaster quietly led the children out of the garden, and Su Tung the Philosopher fell into an honorable sleep. Here endeth the tale of Chung Cheng-

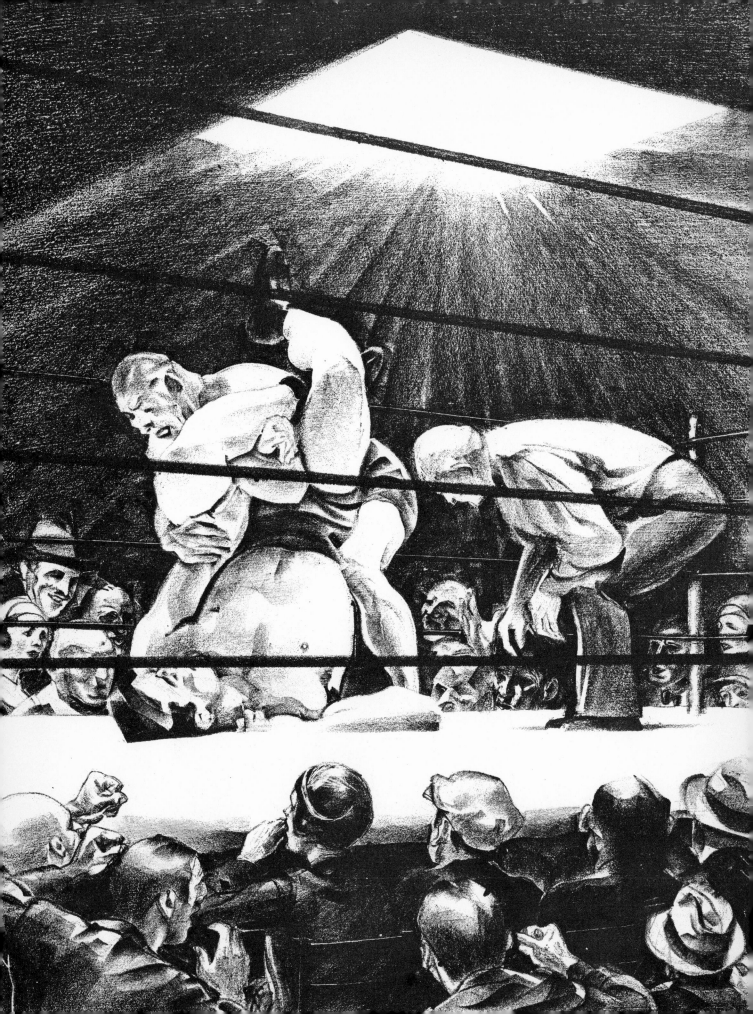

liu, the one-man team from China at the Olympic Games of 1932 in Los Angeles, U.S.A.

To finish off with a wide flourish, there will be exposed a report of sports around the world. Dated, of course. The world changes so rapidly in these stirring times that even yesterday's bulletin is definitely dated. This report was submitted by a kind friend who was lucky in that he had time and money enough to girdle the globe in leisurely fashion. He was asked to keep an eye peeled, ashore and afloat, for sports events of any kind and file an account of same at the end of his journey. His complete report ran as follows:

SIR:

The *Cingalese Prince* (Wilmar Finch, Master) cleared from New York for Yokohama with the undersigned on board under instructions to note, observe, and report on various sports activi-

ties encountered, ashore or afloat, on a trip around the world.

I make no mention of sports observed at such ports of call as Galveston, Panama, and San Diego, since they are the sports to be commonly observed in Boston, New York, Philadelphia, Chicago, and points west. On the ship itself, an English freighter, there was shuffleboard and also deck tennis, this last being played every morning with great fury by the captain and three other officers on the boat deck.

There was quite a ceremony about these daily matches. The players solemnly shook hands before starting as though they never had met before in their lives. They shook hands solemnly after the last point had been scored. A steward, in spick-and-span uniform, called off each point as it was scored, and chalked it on a hatch cover. He was as impressive and efficient as Eddie Conlin used to be in the umpire's chair above the championship tennis matches at Forest Hills.

The shuffleboard course was very sporty, because of the fact that a ventilator shaft protruded on one side, making shots very chancey when the ship was listing to port at the urging of wind or wave, of which there was plenty. An apprentice seaman, sent one day to mark out the shuffleboard course, put the scoring numbers in the wrong squares and otherwise made a mess of things. This was a serious breach of naval etiquette, almost a case of barratry. However, the boy came from a good family and his life was spared.

I must get on to Japan but wish to insert here that the captain and chief engineer carried golf clubs with them and the chief engineer daily delivered instructions at mess on how each golf shot should be played. They had a chance to get on some links about once in every three or four months. On this trip they worked in two rounds of golf, one at Singapore and one at Penang. Each time they had to tee up about six A.M., and each time the captain won, doubtless because of the tips on how to play the game supplied by the chief engineer at mess. Thus was the engineer hoist by his own petard, so to speak.

Away in the land of the Japanese where the paper lanterns glow—as Kipling had it—I saw small boys playing baseball

209

almost everywhere. They played very well, and their bright-colored kimonos made it a pretty picture. Possibly the Boston Braves or the St. Louis Browns might attract a greater following if they dressed their players up in such kimonos. Or the Brooklyn Dodgers, of all people!

In Tokyo I hired a rattletrap at two yen (48 cents, American) an hour, and the driver thought he had done a shrewd stroke of business, at that. We passed a beautiful stadium in which a great crowd was watching some foot races. The driver, possibly thinking that I was an American Olympic athlete on tour—just a moment while I flex my mighty muscles—invited me to enter and compete. He said he could arrange it without any trouble. I did not accept the challenge. So much for athletics in Japan.

At Manila I went to see a prize fight, ticket for ringside seat one peso, or 50 cents, American. The first two fights lasted two rounds each, at the expiration of which time the referee tossed the competitors out of the ring because not one of the four involved had landed a blow of any kind. The last fight was billed as a heavyweight contest. I judged from the size of the "heavyweights" that the world-wide depression has hit the Philippine Islands with particular force. Their heavyweights grossed about 125 pounds each on the hoof, gloves included.

There was a good polo game between an army team and the Polo Club of Manila. One great attraction of polo at Manila is that concoctions called Chamberlain gin slings are used for cooling purposes between chukkers, spectators being allowed to cool off that way as well as the players. I held my own with one of the players who was considered locally a very clever fellow in the cooling-off process.

At Surabaya (Java) I saw a Japanese playing tennis with a Dutchman on a hard court by a canal. The little brown brother was winning handily. In Singapore we had the big game. The ship's crew played soccer against a team of Malay boys employed by a British bottling concern. One of the ship's crew was a fellow who carried a pair of football shoes with him at all times, lest he be caught unprepared. He usually gets to play about twice a year. But at every port he dug up the English papers

210

and memorized the scores of the games and the standings of the clubs back home. That was all he talked about on the trip. Well, sad to say, we lost the big game, despite the enthusiastic play of the seaman who always carried his football shoes with him. The Malaya boys trimmed our gallant sailors, 4–2. The crowd witnessing this stirring contest consisted of two Chinese boys, your correspondent, and a Kling who wore what looked like a Roman toga and had his hair done in a "pug," if that's the word. A Kling is a Dravidian and you will find mention made of him in the Rhyme of the Three Great Captains by Kipling, to wit:

"The frigate-bird shall carry my word to the Kling and the Orang-Laut
How a man may sail from a heathen coast to be robbed in a Christian port."

However, we lost honestly enough. Rain came on during the game. I had my rickshaw top put up, so it didn't bother me, and the players were so interested in the game that they didn't know it was raining. I also attended a prize fight in Singapore— two dollars, Straits money, one dollar, American, for a ringside seat—the main bout was between one Graham of the Royal Air Force and Bud Walley, a native fighter. In the sixth round Walley's manager made him "retire," as they said. He had been knocked down profusely and was beginning to come apart at the seams. The British spectators were all done up in boiled shirts and black dinner jackets; very correct. The Malays were in sarongs, very much the worse for wear. As soon as the main bout was halted, the Malays went outside and completed the fistic program of the night among themselves, about twenty bouts being in progress as I threaded my way off in the dusk.

Because of a touch of the sun in the Malacca Straits, I lost interest in athletics from there on. I saw a billiard match in the Seamen's Club in Penang between two of our ship's officers. Around the table were four passengers, the supercargo and thirty-two bottles of beer. At Colombo, Ceylon, it was pointed out to me that the former insane asylum was now the government office building and nobody noticed the difference. I think I saw a wrestler in Port Said. I fled at once, but the incident so distressed me that I kept my eyes closed for the remainder of the trip.

Yours in part,

(Signed) SINBAD JR.

A rather sketchy report, that, and the intention was to send the confounded chap back over the course again to fill in the immense gaps; but he put in a plea that once around was enough and, as for sports, the United States furnished as much as any one could wish to see. He may be right. So the report was accepted as read. On which note, a motion to adjourn is in order.

AND IN CONCLUSION

Some day a truthful golfer will declaim in accents bold:
"I got the best of all the breaks; ten horseshoe putts I holed;
My wildest hooks and slices bounded back upon the line;
My lucky 87 should have been a 99!"

Some day a baseball manager will fold his arms and say:
"That umpire has an eagle eye; he called 'em right today;
We lost four close decisions and we lost the blinking game;
But I'm sure that he is honest, and I thank him just the same."

Some day a beaten fighter, as he tumbles to the floor,
Will mutter from the resin-dust: "This weakness I deplore,
But he certainly caressed me with a sweet one to the chin.
He's a better man than I am, by the shade of Gunga Din!"

And all these things will come to pass that I have written here.
Though you may laugh a bitter laugh or sneer a wicked sneer.
I've watched the world grow better and—some leeway to allow—
I judge these things will happen just a million years from now.

FINIS